Ode to Life!

as told to Gordon Richiusa

Copyright © 2020
ISBN 978-0-98299-268-5

All rights reserved. No part of this publication may be reproduced, stored in a retrieval system, or transmitted in any form or by any means, electronic, mechanical, recording or otherwise, without the prior written permission of the author(s) or their assigns.

Published in the United States by
Five Birds Publications,
For Heroes' Hearts® Inc.
8112 Terracotta Gulf Ct. Las Vegas NV 89143

This book is not intended as libelous, slanderous or to caste a negative pall on any person either living or dead, except perhaps Hitler and other convicted, unrepentant Nazis criminals. The story is completely derived from first person recorded interviews of Eveline and Eddy Hoffman. Any opinions or statements made by the characters, therefore are the sole responsibility of the survivors. To that end, some names and scenes have been modified to protect the innocent, or those wishing and deserve to remain anonymous.

Edited by Suzanne Hoffman & Barbara Rich
Research and interview notes donated by Shawn Wehan
Cover Art: Carla Hoffman, Design: Dana Stamos
Photo of Michelle Manu, donated by Lynda Lee Photo

Ode to Life!

as told to Gordon Richiusa

Foreword
From the Writer

Here was my problem:
I needed to present two storytellers' voices in one story at the same time, in a manner that would make both sense to the reader as well as keep their interest. I knew as a storyteller that I needed a consistent voice, but sticking simply to the rules of good journalism was just not right, or even *good enough* in this case.

The Hoffmans' story had affected me personally and changed the course of my life. I had to find a way to preserve their rich and detailed memories in the overlapping layers that I was envisioning.

Over the past five decades I have interviewed thousands of people and none of them ever remembered their lives in a straight line from beginning, to middle, to end, episodically like pearls on a strand. Most of the previous stories I've written or re-told have had the foundation of my being a storyteller myself. Often I play a minor role in the stories (as I did in this one) but I always use writing conventions to make everyone's tale easily digestible for the reader. So, you are getting my interpretation of the stories that Eveline and Eddy Hoffman, both Holocaust survivors, shared with me.

They were truly an example of two-hearts-beating-as-one. The value of their story for me was not that it was a

Holocaust story, but because it was a truth-is-stranger-than-fiction example of enduring love.

So, I present the stories in the same manner that they were shared with me, with starts and stops and additions and last second, "Did I ever tell you about..." comments as I was walking out the door. I believe this does not detract from the story, but enhances it and makes it a true *Hoffman* experience.

The fallout of their WWII tragedies are the catalyst for much of the book. However, this is much more than a Holocaust memoir. This is a rich and detailed love story to which all can relate, a story of how two remarkable humans miraculously found one another, how they have worked to heal the scars of their childhoods, and how they have continued to teach redemption and reconciliation through their example. My hope is that my efforts will not turn the Hoffmans' story into a dry lesson about the horrors of war or death. I see this book as an ode to life!

as told to Gordon Richiusa

Eddy and Eveline's Dedication

"The story we're about to tell will surprise you."
--Eddy Hoffman

We make here a solemn dedication to the many survivors and descendants of all ancestry (who, to this day experience the fallout of the Holocaust), and especially to the Jewish descendants of the many, many, many millions of those who were slaughtered.
--Eddy and Eveline Hoffman

[Note: A full statement by Eddy and Eveline appears at the end of this book.]

Ode to Life!

as told to Gordon Richiusa

CHAPTER INDEX

1. Nightmares Have Consequences — p. 11
2. Dreams & Omens — p. 31
3. Winners & Losers — p. 67
4. Illuminating Darkness — p. 89
5. Fire & Ice — p. 121
6. Merry Christmas — p. 133
7. New Life — p. 158
8. Hoffman Was Here — p. 183
9. Business & Pleasure — p. 203
10. The Sweetest Fruit — p. 263
11. Because It Is Healing — p. 277
12. Afterword/Final Statement — p. 317
13. Timeline & Explanation — p. 325
14. Family Photo Gallery — p. 335

Ode to Life!

as told to Gordon Richiusa

Chapter One
Nightmares Have Consequences

The world seemed to slam on its brakes coming to a painful halt. All sound, even the usually unnoticed, background noises of people moving in their chairs, sniffling, coughing, or the drone of the current speaker's voice were muted, unrecognizable. This sudden dome of silence served to amplify Eveline's internal commotions. Her mind and heart were racing uncontrollably. Was this a heart attack? Between the snare drum rapid throb in her ears and the bass drum pounding of her heart, she was suddenly consumed with an internal focus so intense it forced an out-of-body-like awareness of itself. Like a frenzied religious chanting that both accompanies and is guided by a measured deep drone of the cantor, she was both the observer and the observed watching the quakes and shivers reverberate throughout her body like ripples in a pond rebounding occasionally back to the center of her chest.

It was a feeling like none she could remember. While her body seemed ready to burst, she was also calm and detached. Was this a learned behavior, or a tried and true primal defense mechanism that kicked in under extreme life and death moments, which hadn't been used in a long, long time?

If it was learned, how and when did she learn this survival technique? Why did her body and very soul feel the need to respond this way now? Was there any danger? What had caused this reaction?

Fragments of awareness of her immediate surroundings came through her consciousness. She knew where she was and why she was there.

She was just listening to a woman sharing her experiences in a support group for Child Survivors of The Holocaust. A non-distinct person reading a personal recollection in rhyme.

She could no longer hear the reader's voice or make out the words, but the content was clear. Through these words, Eveline could feel with all her senses an unspoken oppressive darkness bearing down on her like a stern but loving hand, keeping the lid on past memories or present dangers from surfacing and perhaps harming. It was a physical sensation of being held down, covered up, silenced. Yet, the quiet was also shrouded by the incessant pounding in her chest, like a shouting voice attempting to break through a veil.

The feeling of being hidden in the dark passed quickly and was replaced by the observation that she was not as frightened as she probably should have been. The physical sensation of a tangible darkness closed in on and enveloped her, surrounding her and almost guiding her to suppress. Suppress what? Her memories? Her feelings? Her hatred? Her anguish? What? The beating of her heart became too loud to contemplate further.

Now, like watching an old home movie of one's life, she observed herself standing up from her drab, grey, folding metal chair. She did not try to stop herself, but felt she needed to act, to DO something. This seemed as good an action as any.

She had to breathe and though she tried to control herself, she took several deep and mournful breaths.

"What am I doing? What is this? Where is this coming from? Who AM I?" Eveline Hoffman heard herself between the rise and fall of heaving sobs and moans that had unexpectedly welled up from some previously unknown depth of her being.

She decided to move toward the door.

*What door? What room? Who **are** these people?* The urgency to answer questions was fading fast.

Eveline felt compelled to try and stay quiet, unseen, watching, but that was a losing battle as new louder groans burst forth from within as she found herself running for a hallway, or perhaps outdoors. It didn't matter.

Whatever was going on, Eveline's only fleeting concern that seemed to make any sense was that she not embarrass her husband Eddy who, she knew, must have been sitting by her side.

This kind of outburst was not only embarrassing and out of character for Eveline, but she didn't want to take attention away from a woman who she now remembered was speaking, telling her own story to the group.

How could she ruin the focus group meeting that she was attending with her husband of 45 years?

He was the Holocaust survivor! He had been a teenager at Auschwitz and moved to another four camps during his imprisonment in WWII.

The Hoffmans were now joining these meetings once a month. They called them *focus groups*. There were only a few rules, one of the most important being: *NO GUESTS allowed*. It had not occurred to Eveline that even she could not have attended as a guest. She thought this stipulation only applied to everyone else. Rightfully so, as at the end of WWII, 720 children who had been orphaned or separated from their parents during the Holocaust had been emigrated to various allied countries when they had been liberated (many eventually ending up in the United States as Eveline and her sisters had). However, Eveline and her sisters were not part of that group. Eddy was.

The English philanthropist Leonard Montefiore had sponsored Eddy's group, but Eveline and thousands of other Jewish children had to follow the same procedures as Eveline's family.

***

No foreigners could come to the U.S.A. BEFORE that time, during the world's unrest, without a request by the government. Eddy was just turning 17 when he was placed in his first orphanage. Three brothers who had been with Eddy in camps also went to Northern Ireland. They were all over 16 but lied so that they could get support.

as told to Gordon Richiusa

***

In this group ***Child Survivors Of The Holocaust*** were brought together to discuss how they were fairing. To Eveline's heartbreak, virtually all of the children (now adults) continued to experience symptoms of trauma.

Eddy and Eveline had been introduced to this group by the video project ***Children of the Shoah***, ***Visual History Foundation*** which was a Steven Spielberg production on behalf of Jewish Holocaust Survivors who were children during their experiences of WWII. Eddy and Eveline met in Cleveland, Ohio where they both had established ties in the U.S..

Eddy was a survivor who had lost every member of his direct family as they were moved into Ghettos and then train cars and finally prison camps with a singleminded precision born out of obsessive hatred.

Eveline had survived due to the quick thinking of her parents who saw a slim opportunity for survival and took it. Eveline and her younger sister Paulette as well as older sister Jacqueline were separated from their parents and smuggled into the countryside in the south of France when the nazis came rolling in with tractors, guns and miles of barbed wire. Eveline and her sisters stayed with a foster family, in hiding until a local Catholic Convent School mother superior ousted the older sister Jacqueline from the convent, after she discovered Jacqueline was Jewish. To save the sisters lives an uncle had offered to sponsor the three girls to the United States.

Eveline was just five years old when her parents, for her and her sisters' safety, had left the three daughters with non Jewish friends on a farm in the south of France. It was safer for the girls to be raised in secrecy from the Nazis and other Jew haters. Eveline did not, at the time, even know what the word Jewish meant. Now, after decades of life, sitting in this place she was starting to understand.

Eveline suddenly felt the gentle presence of someone standing next to her allowing the dark, oppressive silence to include this new person's intrusion like mixing water with wine. It was not her husband. Was it a woman, the speaker? Who?

Eveline had been attending these meetings dutifully to show her support for her husband.

Sometimes those in attendance at the Child Survivors meetings would tell the same stories again and again. Eddy shared many tales, but one story he'd been asked to recall many times in these groups was a dream he'd had prior to being rounded up, that had allowed him a very small sense of safety during his years in the concentration camps.

***

Two weeks prior, a call came to the Palos Verdes home of the Hoffman's which Eveline had answered.

"Hello, Eveline, this is Sarah Moscovitz."

"Hello Sarah," Eveline had responded politely, then added quickly, "Eddy's not here right now."

"That's alright. I'm calling to talk to *you*."

"To me?" asked Eveline.

"Yes, I was wondering why you have not been participating in these groups. You only come to support your husband."

"What do you mean, participate?" asked Eveline.

"Well, you are a Holocaust survivor too," Sarah said simply.

"Me? I was in France during part of the war. I wasn't in any of the camps."

"Yes, but you were with your two sisters. You were in hiding, abandoned by your parents."

"Abandoned?" This word struck a sensitive nerve with Eveline.

Eveline never thought of herself as a Holocaust survivor like her husband who had been in the death camps such as Auschwitz, where he had lost every member of most of his family. She also never considered herself *abandoned*.

Here there were others who had signed on to the Children of the Shoah project, most of whom were orphaned when the Nazis began to implement their horrific extermination plan, focusing mostly on the Jews, as usual.

"Yes, Eveline, you are a Holocaust survivor," Sarah said more emphatically.

Ph.d. Sarah Moscovitz, Author of the book, **Love Despite Hate** then made a special phone invitation to Eveline. "Please come to the next meeting with an open mind. I think it will do you good. It seems clear to me that you have suppressed your memories to protect yourself. It's one of the many common mechanisms of PTSD."

"PTSD?" Eveline thought the acronym for Post Traumatic Stress Disorder was also absurd. "But I was just a five year old child when my sisters and I were rescued from France. I'm not a soldier. I didn't lose my parents. We all survived and none of us were in the camps like Eddy.

The conversation ended on a friendly note, without pressure from Sarah.

"Tell Eddy I said hi and hope to see you both next week."

***

Recalling that phone call was a brief, logical intrusion in the chaos raging inside her at that moment. Eveline knew that she was still standing, but felt like she was slowly spiraling backward and not to Earth, but to an awareness of being who she was, Eveline.

As she fluttered closer to the world at hand a familiar but weird darkness came and went, but was closing in again. She felt helpless, as if she was being required to turn her full attention and focus inward on herself. It was a place she had been avoiding, perhaps.

It was as if silence and darkness were an ephemeral cocoon, wings of protection closing and opening as needed. Suddenly the cocoon was being pierced again, not only by the strange sounds emerging from her mouth as her lips parted but by an awareness of another person standing next to her.

Eveline tried to hold back the animal wails that knotted her stomach, accompanied by the throbbing in her heart and head.

Instead of fright, she was experiencing a mixture of shame and even failure as if her sobs would interfere with "real sadness," what she had convinced herself was the actual focus of the group.

So, when it was clear to Eveline that she was not going to regain control of herself, and the details of the circle of chairs were fading away, she gathered up some part of herself and ran for her life clutching her chest as if holding it together.

The present came into focus from the haze of the past and she faced head on, with a new clarity, what was going on inside her. Eveline observed clearly Sarah again.

"I think maybe you were right," Eveline heard what sounded like her own voice speaking to Sarah, in response to the telephone conversation earlier.

At first Sarah's words were indistinct, but Eveline could tell by the tone that what Sarah was saying was not *I told you so* or other words of conflict, but soft, kind, caring, and most of all soothing sounds. The therapist was not admonishing Eveline in any way. Luckily, the dictionary meanings were not important. The words were meant to heal and calm, but Eveline still felt she needed to resist; something kept telling her she was an outsider at these meetings. She did not feel that her experiences were somehow bad enough to call herself a Holocaust Survivor.

"Your wounds have been covered up for a long time. We are here for you, in any way that you like."

Eveline could hear, but did not feel a need to respond.

***

Eveline had always felt that she was very strong as a child because she protected her younger sister, Paulette. But, what had she really done? How had she ever really demonstrated this strength?

She was only five at the time of her abandonment, and it was actually Jacqueline (the eldest of the three) who was given the charge by her parents to, "Take care of your sisters."

Eveline had a full head of thick straight, brown hair with brown-eyes. She was a perfect little French girl. Paulette's hair was a bit thinner and more straight, which she was never happy about. Jacqueline's hair was thick and wavy which Eveline always thought was very pretty.

In truth, Eveline had convinced herself that she could never be 100% sure if she was remembering perfectly her time with her sisters in hiding. Her *memories* might be nothing more than her imagination filling in the forced forgetfulness of childhood trauma with images that her older sister had planted there.

However, there was no argument that Eveline and her family had suffered, from the moment the Nazis had made their first move toward desensitizing the Jews and rounding them up for slaughter.

Eveline's mother had given to her the Star of David that she and all Jews were forced to wear in Vichy France. Not only did each Jewish person have to endure inhumane treatment beyond the scope of their imaginations, but they had to make their own stars for easy identification.

Jacqueline, the older sister's memoir descriptions had always had the feel of memory and seemed very real right at this moment. As she stood in a traumatic haze, Eveline drifted in and out of the past.

It was as if she suddenly could feel, see and hear the sounds of her youth. Eveline and her sister Paulette, under the wing of the eldest Jacqueline, the cloth of the Patois guides' uniform on her face as she and Paulette rode on the backs of Freedom Fighters over The Pyrenees like the Von Trapp family in *The Sound Of Music*.

In 1940 the Nazi's invaded France. One year prior, in 1939 Britain and France had allied once again and declared war on Germany. Failed strategies aside, Eveline's parents knew that every Jew needed to leave as soon as possible before being gathered up and sent to concentration camps. Her parents had decided to try a dangerous escape route to Spain, but knew that it was too dangerous for children. The plan was that the children would be put into hiding briefly and that they all would be reunited later when a safer route could be determined. The original plan was never fully implemented and it was two years later, after living in hiding the entire time that Eveline's Uncle Harry sponsored his nieces' escape to the U.S.A. By now, the situation was even more dire.

So, on Christmas Eve, 1942 under cover of darkness, the three girls were taken to meet the Patois (mountain people) who were well paid and would take them over the Pyrenees Mountains into Spain.

The date was chosen deliberately because everyone knew that the border guard posts would not be heavily staffed on Christmas Eve.

At the meeting with the Patois other children were also present, all waiting to cross to relative safety.

The lead guide, a man Eveline remembered as being Monsieur Jean spoke quietly in French, but with urgency to the children, "This is going to be a very dangerous crossing. We will be moving on foot all night. You will get tired, but you cannot lay down to rest. If you do, you will die. We cannot stop for any reason." Then to the older children, "You must follow the guide in front of you. Step only in his tracks! Do not make new ones. If someone sees that we have any children with us it will attract dangerous attention."

The three year old sister, Paulette was given warm wine so she would sleep. Both Paulette and Eveline were carried on the backs of the guides, but Jacqueline at 10 had to walk. All the children had been directed to put on their warmest clothes and to stuff newspapers into their boots for insulation.

as told to Gordon Richiusa

Eveline clung tightly to her guide's back. She remembered thinking, "It's so cold. There is so much snow everywhere. I'm tired. I want my *maman*. The shadows are frightening. Nobody is talking, just walking, walking."

As soon as the group was on their silent way, Eveline looked over the shoulder of her guide and noticed that Paulette's shoe was missing. It had fallen off somewhere in the snow and got left behind. Eveline worried about the danger to the group that this might arouse, "Will dogs now find us?"

Monsieur Jean had told them, "Any guards on duty will be watching. Make no sound because it carries far in the mountains. We must avoid the many Gestapo checkpoints. Sometimes they have bloodhounds that not only can smell fear, but the slightest sound can give us away."

Eveline's main concern however, was for the welfare of her sisters. "Will Paulette's foot freeze? Is this walk too hard for Jacquline?"

At one point, Jacqueline had wanted to relieve herself but was not allowed. Eveline had always felt that this was a deeply humiliating experience for her sister that she might never forget.

Soon, the slope on the hillside became steep and harder to climb. The group proceeded slowly for a few more hours, then with a signal of his hand, Monsieur Jean had everyone stop. The first Gestapo guard post was close and he wanted to make all the children aware how critical it was to remain silent. No one made a sound. It was extremely cold. The freezing snow fell and seemed to muffle the sounds of feet on the march. Before dawn, two more guard posts were passed, the group remained unseen. Just before first light, the guards seemed to relax and the passage went without incident as they neared the Spanish border checkpoint.

Finally, Monsieur Jean pointed at some lights in the distance and proclaimed, "Barcelona."

"*Don't trust anyone* but Jacqueline," someone had once directed Eveline, probably her mother, when they were just about to leave each other's company. Eveline remembered that she must never mention her mother or father to anyone, or that they were *Jewish,* but Eveline didn't really know what that meant. The cautionary direction stayed with Eveline the rest of her life and she always felt guarded, especially around those she just met who were not Jewish.

Even now, not really knowing what or where Barcelona was, she looked at Jacqueline for verification that what the guide had pointed at was somehow an important truth. Jacqueline slowly was marching in the direction that Monsieur had pointed, and her step seemed to pick up a bit. Eveline relaxed.

The group arrived at what appeared a final destination just before sunrise, on Christmas Day, near the town of La Molina. At first, Eveline thought this was the end of the trek, but no. There was more travel.

After a two day recuperation, the children were piled into a mule cart and after another rendezvous, taken down the other side of the mountains. The mule cart wound its way down. When it neared the Catalonia seaport, Eveline and her sisters looked out the window and saw her parents standing on the platform. "Maman! Papa!"

The details of all these images flashed through Eveline's head at the very thought of the word, *abandoned*

In the mixed up emotions of the moment, Eveline could not remember ever really feeling hungry when she was left with a foster family. Though she also began feeling like there was a giant hole at her center that could never be filled, and this may have played a role in her adult behavior.

When she was torn from her mother and left with a farming family who were *not relatives,(a couple who was* willing to care for the girls and *could be trusted)* Eveline always knew that she'd be reunited, because that is what her *maman* and *papa* had told her. The woman she was left with at first was Josie, Eveline's father's business associate's wife. That's why Eveline bristled at the word, *abandoned*. Eveline had read many of the same or similar images that Jacqueline had written about in her memoir, "Chased by Demons."

***

In April of 1943 Eveline had come to the U.S. by way of Portugal, much like the refuges in the classic movie **Casablanca** except that she was a child, not Ingrid Bergman. About 60 children had followed a convoluted path, from train station to train station, port to port, vessel to vessel until finally, out of Portugal aboard the **Sera Pinta**, she and the other children along with a few adults took the 2 week voyage that brought her to America.

An Uncle, Harry and his wife Caroline came to meet the three sisters when their ship arrived. Uncle Harry and his wife had agreed to sponsor the girls trip to safety to the United States; And, though they met the three girls at the docks when they arrived, after seeing them, (and probably at the insistence of Eveline's aunt) the couple had decided that they could *not* keep the children. So, they made arrangements with the Jewish Family Service to take them to Belfair Orphanage in Cleveland, Ohio even though the girls were not orphans.

The girls' parents, Simon and Anna had survived with the resistance somehow, but there was no hope that they would be allowed to join their girls in the United States any time soon. Simon had saved enough money and had made enough connections that kept he and Anna safe in Barcelona until the family could be reunited. So, the orphanage decided to allow the girls to stay with them until suitable foster parents could be found.

Mostly, Eveline could remember how proud she felt when her parents met the girls at a dock outside Philadelphia. Looking around proudly, as if other children could see her she thought, "See, I told you I am not an orphan!"

In the first foster home, the wife was physically abusive to Eveline and Paulette. Jacqueline had found a suitable foster home soon after arriving, nearby where her younger sisters were placed. Jacqueline found out about this abuse from neighbors and when she visited her younger sisters, she saw bruises. Still only eleven years old, she told the social worker and demanded her sisters be removed from foster care until a new family could be found. At that point, Paulette and Eveline were returned briefly to Belfair Orphanage until a second foster family could be found.

Shortly thereafter, Adolph and Ida Weintraub took in the two younger girls. Ida couldn't have children of her own and wanted to do what she could for *the cause*. Adolph owned a gas station. He was always grimy under his nails. The only time he raised his hand to the girls in his care was once when Eveline dared him to do it. He gently tapped her arm and she was devastated because she adored him and felt very safe with both of the Weintraubs.

It was in this second foster home that Eveline began to exhibit signs of trauma. One of the favorite manufactured foods of the time was Tip Top Bread. It was also called Cotton Bread by Eveline's father and was a lot like Wonder Bread. After an early dinner at the Weintraubs, Eveline stole a full loaf and hid it under her bed for comfort. She had the idea that she would be able to eat the bread later, worrying she might be hungry during the night.

This plan did not go well as Ida found the loaf the very next morning. Eveline was terrified that she was going to be punished as she had at the first foster home, but Ida was loving and did not say anything about the bread.

It was not unlike Ida to strike the girls from time to time though, sometimes more than once, with a small piece of green garden hose. Still Eveline and Paulette felt safe and cared for. They lived in this home for about three years until Simon and Anna were allowed to emigrate and got an apartment on the same street as the Weintraubs. In the same apartment building, Ida's best friend and her husband (Ruth and Bill) lived upstairs.

"Let me show you something really important in the basement," Bill said to a trusting nine year old Eveline one day. She followed trustingly.

When they went into the basement, without a moment's hesitation he started rubbing himself against the young Eveline. Instantly, instinctively feeling this was wrong, she started screaming, pushed him away, and ran upstairs to Ida. Eveline was very strong for her age which probably stopped the attack from proceeding. Hysterically, Eveline found Ida who never seemed to question the truth of Eveline's accusation. Ida calmed her down with soft words and hugs. "Don't worry," Ida said when Eveline was able to breath without gasping. "Don't worry, I'll take care of it."

Bill never bothered Eveline again.

***

Seeing her husband sitting there beside her in the car as they drove from the meeting had a somewhat calming affect on Eveline. Eddy had always been able to take control of every situation with just his presence. And, though Eveline was relieved that Eddy was sitting next to her now, his gentle smile and the echo of Sarah Moskowitz's words also triggered conflicting feelings of an overwhelming sense of elation that she and her husband were some of the very few "lucky ones" while at the same time almost a sadness and guilt for not doing, saying, or trying more to honor the millions who were not so lucky.

"We're home now," Ed said as he parked the car in the driveway of their home. He moved quickly around to the passenger door to open it for his wife. The ride home seemed to bring her slowly back to the stability of Earth.

It would ordinarily have taken one hour, but now the ride seemed to have spanned decades.

Ode to Life!

as told to Gordon Richiusa

Chapter Two
Dreams & Omens

After Eveline had her traumatic event and was working through her feelings and memories, there was a gentle knock followed by a gong-like bell. She went to the front door.

Eddy had gone to the Jewelry facility, and when Eveline opened the door there stood Maureen, a neighbor and friend, cradling a toaster in her arms like a sleeping baby.

"Hi Evie," she said. "I hope I'm not bothering you, but I just got a new toaster to match my new granite countertops and this one is perfectly good. I didn't want to throw it out. Do you want a fairly new toaster?"

Eveline remembered the extreme effort it took not to show the shock and dismay that she felt at that moment. The toaster's brand name was facing forward, toward Eveline. It read, "Krups", which could just as well have been a Nazi swastika as a name.

The innocent neighbor did not know that the Krupp family had been on trial at Nuremberg. The neighbor did not know that Eddy Hoffman had been the slave labor of this and other companies.

Ode to Life!

The Krupp company was just one of many, who knew of and supported the policy of forced slave labor as a smart business decision. The Nazis wanted to exterminate the Jews and others. They didn't care how they were killed. If Krupp and others wanted to *work* the Jews to death, so be it. The Krupp family had dropped the second "P" and added an "S" after the war to try and escape their past.

***

Eddy's parents Josef and Szeren Hoffman (Sara in English) showed *Bumi* (as they called their son) a great deal of attention. Not that he was made soft by babying or over attention, but even he could see at this young age of eight that he was precious in his parent's eyes.

His parents had lost their first son before Eddy (Bumi) was born, an older brother who had died in one of the many circumstances that was called a *crib death* at the time, and so Eddy was the oldest in the household and inherited both privilege and responsibility.

At this time, Bumi was eight years old. His hair dark brown. However, when he was born until about one year earlier, Eddy's hair was white. This included his eyebrows and eyelashes.

The town where he grew was called Nagyszöllös—which means "large grapevines"—and true to its name it was a city of wine, nestled in the foothills of the Carpathian Mountains of Central Europe, where Hungary, Ukraine and Slovakia converge. This peaceful valley community was at the base and to the right on a relief map of towering mountains. It was part of an eastern province that, in the early twentieth century still belonged to the Austro-Hungarian Monarchy.

The teeming and vibrant Carpathian mountain range was the third longest on the European Continent and put Eddy's family—led by patriarch Josef Hoffman, Eddy's father—close to the Romanian border.

***

Szeren Frid was a woman ahead of her time. In 1924, at the ripe old age of seventeen, she decided she wanted to attend the University of Budapest. This, in itself was unusual. However, her parents had money and did not allow their daughter to be disappointed.

She met Josef one evening in 1926 at a boxing match. Eddy's father was a professional boxer and was on the fight card at a local meeting hall. Szeren waited after the bouts were concluded and boldly introduced herself to the young boxer Josef Hoffman. Shortly after she graduated, the two of them wed. The caveat was that Josef was already promised to someone else. Family history told of Josef leaving his betrothed at the alter, so that he could marry Szeren. The 1st fiancé never married and always treated Eddy as if he were her own child.

At the end of 1927 the first Hoffman boy was born, but he passed away prior to his first birthday. Eddy was born in February of 1929, as often was the case, to stunt Szeren's sorrow of losing her first child. Szeren (known in the translation as Sara) did not want Josef to continue fighting after they were wed. However, Josef kept his gloves and other training equipment and Sara did not object to his teaching his sons how to box.

Eveline, in later years was convinced that Eddy's seemingly super punching power was from these early lessons.

***

Josef's family ancestors had lived in the fertile region since early in the sixteenth century. What began as a single homestead, had since blossomed into the Hoffman Farm, then a cluster of houses that was later known officially as the Hoffman *Falau* or Villageafter that. There was always a slight distinction between what constituted a village, town, or city.

***

Since the creation of the concept of *nations*, human beings in these lands were trying to live a peaceful life. Where Czechoslovakia, Germany, Hungary, Romania, and Russia converged, there had been many conflicts by power seekers.

The Hungarian culture and language had an interesting history, as the people of this culture had a very close association to the Mongolians. There were no pronouns for gender, no *he* or *she* designations. The Yiddish that was spoken by the Jews was a mix of 15th century German, so it could not be easily translated into modern German. When Eddy was enslaved, the German soldiers were not able to understand what the Jewish prisoners were saying or writing, but the prisoners could easily translate and understand the German language.

***

For five hundred years, the Hoffman clan had strengthened their reputation as a respected farming and business family in the modest and peaceful agricultural community.

It was here that Eddy learned by example to accept the many responsibilities that life would put upon him as a male Hoffman.

There had always been a desire for male babies on these farms. There was however, a tradition of the men actively caring for the women to the point of self sacrifice, probably because women were the only ones who were equipped for the miracle of childbirth. Regardless, in the Hoffman clan, boys were the rule rather than the exception. So Eddy only had brothers and mostly uncles. Boy or girl however, this farmland was a perfect setting for a child growing up

Throughout the country, there was still a lot of pride in the fact that Attila The Hun was born from this same Hungarian stock. Ironically, while most school children in the area knew pertinent details of Attila's conquests, it always seemed a source of pride to the Hungarians that he had beaten the Italians and protected the Homelands from the Romans and many other countries.

Clear snow from the mountains fed streams into the River Tisza, which helped create the fertile soil that made this region an ideal place for Eddy's forefathers to raise children and nurture their agro-business legacy.

Every morning the eight year old Bumi started his chores by picking up fruit from the ground that had fallen from the family orchards during the night. At eight, Bumi had discerned that the sweetest fruit was always that which fell from the trees. If this ripe fruit was allowed to stay on the ground, of course it would be eaten by other animals or insects and quickly rot to become unfit for human consumption. If he was lucky, he would not need to climb a ladder or tree or use any heavy (for an eight year old) poles to pick the fruit he needed for the family. Every day he'd return with a sufficient amount that would cause all to remark, *"I don't know how he does it! Bumi sure knows how to pick the sweetest fruit!"*

For some reason a neighbor's fruit was even better in Eddy's young mind and he often wandered across imaginary boundaries and physical fences to reap the bounty of proverbial greener pastures on the other side. Naturally, all the local farmers knew what was happening, but instead of complaining they smiled at Eddy's ingenuity.

There was a close sense of community throughout the region, but especially locally. For example, each family was responsible for cutting their own wood, which was used for heating as well as cooking. The unwritten and unquestioned rule was that when a family cut down a tree, they would have to plant a sapling in it's place. This maintained an ecological balance long before forestry was even a consideration.

Later, after Eddy's liberation from the death/slave camps, the Russians (who had absorbed the region) came and chopped down all the trees with no replacements, which caused flooding and devastation throughout all the local villages. Unluckily, the homes were made of adobe, which is clay (mud) mixed with straw.

***

By today's standards life was pioneer-primitive. There was no refrigeration, for instance as there was no electricity, no gas, and no phones. To keep foods cold they were placed into a bucket and dropped down deep into the well, left to hover just above the water to keep cold. Many conveniences that we now think of as commonplace were simply not available and no one really missed them.

In fact, young Eddy made a game out of every chore. He liked to feed the chickens, naming every one, and talking to the roosters, about new enterprises he felt might help out his family.

One day, after milking time was done, Eddy witnessed as always, everyone letting their cows out onto the street to join the herd as the procession wandered into the hills for the day.

It was a procession that was followed closely by a herder in the back of the line. The herder was preceded slightly by a bull who knew that it was his job to protect the females of the herd. He walked behind the group, big head held high and alert. Scanning left and right. If the bull could have smiled or let a sigh of satisfaction, he probably would have.

Since protection of the cows was taken care of, one of the associated jobs of the herder was making sure that the cows did not stop and graze on large clumps of clover that grew in the fields, but might be easily accessed along the roadway. This had long fascinated Eddy.

Fresh, uncooked clover, like no other plant gave the cows gas, and this caused the cows to blow up like balloons, a problem with any of the grazing cows. This build up of gas was dangerous and could kill the grazing cattle. If this happened, drastic measures had sometimes to be taken, and the local veterinarian was sent for. The most expedient method of cow gas relief was to stick a large knife into the offending stomach. In the case of cows, there are a total of four compartments in the stomach to aid in digestion. When they were cut, which seldom happened, the sound of air escaping and the sound of a sharp knife piercing the stomach of the cows was something that had always stayed with Eddy.

All killing of the farm animals was done in the traditional, kosher way, a point that was well made one time when Eddy faced his arch nemesis: a family goose. When he was small, he was often chased and spat upon by a particularly aggressive gander. Eddy Hoffman's grandmother kept flocks of geese, chickens and occasionally other fowl. The collection of eggs were a daily ritual, as was milking. Often this particular foul tempered goose would chase young Bumi all the way to the door of his house where his grandmother would have to intervene. Perhaps it was this ongoing feud that usually allowed Eddy to be assigned to other chores, but one day he was asked to go into the pen where the geese were kept and let them out to roam the property looking for food. When Eddy opened the gate the goose charged right at him and took a bite out of his behind. Geese and other birds are often used as a first line security system. This time, however, Bumi had enough and grabbed the goose by the neck and with a swift twist killed it.

His sense of righteous dignity was not satisfied with the taking of this one life. While the first goose was still warm, Ed went on a rampage. His anger had reached a peak. He caught and killed six or seven geese in the pen.

When he returned to the house to immediately confess his deed to his father, Eddy offered this suggestion, by way of minimizing the senseless slaughter. He said, "Well, at least we can eat them."

"No," his father pointed out sternly but softly. "These geese cannot be eaten by our family. They were not killed in a kosher manner."

"What should we do with them?" Eddy asked.

"Not we, but YOU will take the geese to our non-Jewish neighbors and sell or trade them for what you can get. If you need to, give them as gifts. You have to do this today. I don't want dead geese in our pen."

Ode to Life!

Bumi got rid of all the dead geese, placing them into a small wooden cart and wheeling them to the neighbors.

***

The third and fourth male Hoffmans, Bumi's brothers Karl and Tibor came shortly after but at this early date, Bumi was enjoying an idyllic life as the favored child on a farm that was directly related to his ancestors.

From as early as Eddy could remember, his father and grandfather would concoct daily rituals and tests which were presented simply as, "The way we Hoffmans do things." An example of these special rituals luckily only came in the winter months when the men and boys would be rousted from their beds early before dawn and taken out into the snow. In the high mountains, snows fell and stayed through several months of the year. The males would be led outside where they would strip almost naked to the skin and basically bathe in the snow drifts. Eddy couldn't remember when these snow baths had started, but he and his cousins and then his brothers would all without question start most of their winter days in this manner. Eddy noticed that if one vigorously rubbed the snow on every part of the body, from head to toe, a kind of radiating warmth would soon overtake the chill.

Eddy's given name was Adolf after his grandfather. The nickname, Bumi was the most familiar way that everyone let him know that he was special and may have contributed to Eddy's interest in turning everything into an enterprise. Sometimes, in the course of a day, Eddy would wander into the town to see what opportunities he could find there.

If he arrived early enough he would see all of the shop owners sweeping up the area in front of the individual shops before it was time to open. This was an activity that was mandated by the local government, and not cleaning your space could lead to fines.

One day young Hoffman had wandered into town and was watching a shop owner as he received a stern warning from the local police.

"I'm sorry," he was saying. He had been ill and missed a day of cleaning.

"That's not our problem," the policeman had told the shop owner. "Next time, you'll be cited." They left the shop owner with broom in hand and his head hanging low in shame.

"I could ·help you with this," young Hoffman came forward when the police had departed.

"You? How?" asked the shop owner.

"I will come here every morning, before you open and clean your area in front of your store. I'll do it for..." a slight pause..."a pengorr (about 2 1/2 dollars) a week."

So a bargain had been struck and dutifully, every morning no matter the weather, Eddy would clean the area in front of this man's store. Soon, other shop owners saw what was happening and they too hired Ed for the same amount. Young Hoffman reasoned that it was just as easy to clean all the stores on one side of a street as it was to clean just one. Now, of course his 2 *pengorr* a week's enterprise had turned into a full-scale operation.

All this was unknown to his family. All they knew was that Eddy's chores were always done on time and perfectly. All other times of the day it was assumed he was "just growing up." They could depend on him.

So, no one faulted Eddy when, at the twilight-end of one particular day he had stopped at his grandmother's (Babi) house to rest, eat, and spend the night. Walking all the way to his father's house was more than Bumi could face, and grandma made all family members feel welcome.

On this night several others had also taken refuge at Grandma's a small house in Village Hoffman. On this night Eddy had a dream that would define and help his salvation over the next few years of his life.

Like most children, dreams were always vivid, colorful, and magical, so this dream was all the more memorable because it was none of these things.

On this night he had a dream. It was the same dream he would have two days later, etching clearly in his consciousness.

Eddy found himself in a dreary, black and grey landscape. There was no color, no sound. At first he was alone but then sensed that others were also nearby. Looking up he saw several faces coming into view right in front of him.

There were clearly two directions in the dreamscape. First was where all the others were coming from, stepping into the dream. The other was behind him. The faces of the others seemed strained, terrified, looking over Eddy's head to a place behind him. It was as if something behind was pulling or pushing his attention. There were only men, no women.

As he turned he saw a huge, double sided, iron gate that reached high above the heads of his dream companions. The gates were open but suddenly, he watched in horror as the gates that were behind him, now in front started to close. He could no longer move to run, or turn to see the others behind him. Slowly the gates were closing and though there was still no sound, he felt the others were troubled, terrified as the iron gates slammed shut. Suddenly, now he realized that he could move but was trapped along with everyone else behind these huge iron gates. Then there was a new awareness. He had become paper thin! This was fortuitous because now he could easily pass through a slit between the bars that was still visible just as they were closing. It was as if he'd become like an envelope that could float easily through the slot on a mailbox. He slipped through!

When he turned around, he saw many heads floating above the iron gates. They were still almost faceless, but he felt he knew them. They were somehow familiar, his people, his town, his family.

He tried to cry for these faceless bodies, but the tears would not come. The gates closed completely now with a loud clanking sound, as sound had apparently returned to the dream.

Eddy found himself on one side and all the others of his people that he ever knew or would know on the other. The light of their faces began to flicker and the images grew dim, even more grey and colorless than before. Suddenly, in the course of dream-time, little Eddy found himself alone, totally and completely alone. This was not a comfortable feeling.

It's hard to know what such a dream could mean, but a few nights later he had the same dream once again.

He was tired that night. He had finished sweeping the front porches of the storefronts in town before school that morning. Never allowing himself to be satisfied even with a clear success, Eddy had decided to parlay his earnings beginning with a single bag of taffy. He took these and sold each piece at school for about double what he was earning for sweeping a porch. A boy had to make a living.

His pockets were often over full, so he would buy some bread or other item for the family with his earnings.

On this night, he again decided to stop at his grandmothers house. Eddy yawned, said hello, gave his grandmother some food from his stash and crawled into bed, nestled next to his younger brothers, Karl and Tibor who were also sleeping over.

He hoped that he wouldn't have the disturbing dream again. He didn't like it.

Unfortunately, as soon he fell asleep the dream repeated. He was floating, helpless, moving with the crowd. He sensed he wasn't alone. Stirring slightly he felt Karl and Tibi floating near him this time but he couldn't reach out for them, or move in their direction.

Why wouldn't anyone help him, he wondered? Where was his mother, his father, his grandfather? He couldn't find any of them in the sea of bodies, all floating toward the large iron gates. They were ominous, black, large, impenetrable. Everyone was being herded inside...by whom?

Eddy looked around but didn't recognize anyone. He lost sight of his two brothers. Again, he was left completely alone.

As he turned to watch the gates close this time, he suddenly could move. He again became paper thin and slipped through the gates just as they were about to slam shut. When he turned around, he saw so many heads, as before, floating above the iron gates. They were faceless but Ed somehow knew that they were his people, people of his town, his family.

Again he tried to cry but the tears still would not come. The gates closed with a huge clanking sound. The iron gate was giant and as it closed behind him, he again found himself on one side and his entire family on the other. He was alone, totally and completely alone.

When he awoke, he never told anyone about the reoccurring dream. Who would listen, who would believe

Ode to Life!

him? What would he say? He didn't even know what it meant, nor would mean. He had porches to sweep and taffy to sell.

His thoughts wandered to a little red pigtailed girl and he wondered if she would look at him at school tomorrow. "Maybe I will put her pig tails in the ink well, and then I might steal an apple from my neighbor's tree on the way home," he thought to himself.

Soon, without much effort the dream was forced from his mind and he was glad to be back in the comforting arms of reality, though there was an uncomfortable residual, uneasiness that stayed with Eddy the rest of the day.

***

By this time, he had expanded on his taffy selling enterprise and carried his merchandise to school. where he'd made enough money along with his sweeping to feel that he could help support his family. When his father offered him an allowance at this time, Eddy told his father that he did not need it and gave his dad the details of the new taffy enterprise. His father's eyes gleamed with pride. One day he had another idea for expansion and told his friend Isadore--who had joined the conglomeration. "Isadore," he said to his friend, "Let's go to the base and sell to the soldiers."

"Huh?" Isadore wondered. Wouldn't it be dangerous to go to the base?"

"No," Eddy told him. "We can take the money we're making with taffy and buy post cards for the soldiers. We can get stamps for them, too. The soldiers must be homesick and want to write to their families. Post cards cost half a pengorr, but the soldiers would probably be happy to get them. Eddy was right, and soon he and Isadore were successfully operating a multilevel marketing plan.

Eddy, as usual turned out to be absolutely correct in his savvy business thinking.

The soldiers were happy to pay a small amount for postcards, and they also wanted candies to send or carry along with the cards. The taffy came in handy at this point. Eddy and Isadore sold a postcard and taffy kit for a little bit more.

The money that Eddy and Isadore started to make was beginning to surpass the amount Ed made merely sweeping the porches of storefronts. However, that didn't stop Ed from continuing to do the morning chores which now included cleaning the storefronts.

***

Eddy's father was born in 1901 and his mother in 1907. Josef Hoffman was a partisan, also known as a guerrilla fighter during the war. He was like an underground fighter. Eddy's mother was a college graduate. She had gone to University of Budapest for her degree.

It was unusual for women to be educated during this time in history, but Eddy's mother was very unusual. She was also beautiful with jet-black hair and green eyes. By the time she was 36, she was running the family business and taking care of three children.

Eddy's parents owned a manufacturing business and they supplied shoes to the local hospital. Both neighbors and people from far away came to buy his father's specialty, orthopedic shoes. He even made boots for the local military and police.

***

In 1942 Josef Hoffman, Eddy's father was drafted by the Hungarian government. The Jews were not really part of the fighting. They were not allowed to join the military. They were conscripted, as often happened in world history, the Jews were needed to be a labor force. In fact, many great leaders had Jewish counselors, scientists, strategists.

In this story Eddy's father was drafted to support the military operation, but not be a soldier. The Hungarian Military, the Romanian Military, and the Italian military were attached to the German forces. They were called the Axis Forces. The Jewish workers, who were called *Munkas Tabor*, which meant the working class, not considered in anyway equal to the Germans, or even totally human by the Nazis' standards.

When the Russians encountered Romanian, Hungarian, Italian, or German soldiers, they fought them. The people in this area really could not care less about which kind of government took ownership of their lands, as long as they were able to live, work, enjoy their lives. Sometimes though they took sides when they felt that basic humanity was at stake.

***

So, after being drafted, Josef went AWOL and joined the *partisans*, who were anyone who wasn't Russian who wanted to fight on the Russian side. That's when he became an enemy of the Axis forces. Josef's whole company had been shipped out to the Russian front. Some of the men who came back to the Village (discharged) told Eddy's family that Josef had joined the partisan's when he went AWOL. The partisans were fighting the Germans and therefore so was Josef. In many people's minds including Bumi's, it was all very confusing. He knew however that his father--as his grandfather had been--was a good man and often made his decisions based more upon principle rather than economics.

From what Eddy remembered in his later years, his life on the farm was very good, the family business was successful and his father was a local leader in the community, a leader of the Socialist party. Papa Josef was best friends with the mayor of the town and the chief of police. Neither one of his father's friends were Jewish. That didn't matter before the war.

The Russian Army always tried to strike at their enemy's weakest point because it was easier to break through a fortified line when the military's heart was not in the battle. The Italian and Romanian language were more Latin based than the Germans and their temperaments were also different. That's why, when the Americans advanced into Europe the Italian and Romanians gave up easily.

Ode to Life!

Then came March 15, 1939. The Hungarian Army, allied with Germany's Third Reich, marched across the country and into the Hoffman town.

***

The Germans were not ready to have a world war at this time. The British, always ready to negotiate (for peace or for war) came over and tried to negotiate a peace treaty using Neville Chamberlain acting as administer of the process. The Russians wanted to make peace and offered their man, Molotov, to speak for Stalin. After a few months, a pact was made to split Poland in half. Poland had made a pact with the Western countries and the Russians also got to take a part of Eastern Poland and the Germans took possession of north western Poland.

About this time the Hungarians had claimed the mountains of this Carpathian region, and parts of Romania as their ancient Hungary.

Modern Hungary was whittled down, therefore to a very small country by comparison. Hungarians took back part of Romania after WWI.

During WWI (1914-1918) all parties were too confident that they could take care of themselves. They were wrong in many cases, so there was a lot of room for atonement.

***

What many do not realize is that Slovakia is still in existence today and once the sole sovereign in the region.

The Danube starts in Northern Europe and crosses many countries.

as told to Gordon Richiusa

***

Jews had always considered Israel to be their homeland in the Middle East, but the region was always in flux, so without a land to call home, they often spread to and settled in the most fertile lands.

In the 1500s Spain was also a world power. The royalty of Spain, became Catholic Christians and the persecution of anyone not Catholic (including Jews and Muslims) spawned the Dark Ages and the Spanish Inquisition.

The Slavic people were more comfortable in a communal society. Yugoslavia eventually became completely communist under Tito. However, Stalin and Tito did not get along well after WWII. Petty, personal issues were often at the core of international disputes.

In 1939 the Polish army was allowed to cross into Carpathia to get away from the German army. They realized they could not win against the Germans. The Germans told the Hungarians to allow them to leave. There were no shots fired, but Eddy remembers, as a child seeing truckloads of Polish soldiers crossing though his homeland, unimpeded by the Hungarian army.

The Polish Army eventually ended up in England fighting with the British. The purpose of attacking Poland was to prevent domination by the Soviet Union, as Russia was on one side of Poland and Germany on the other.

***

At the end of WWII Carpathia became Ukraine, and Slovakia stayed as it was. Chamberlin was called in again, hoping to appease the instigators of the last two wars, gave part of Czechoslovakia--something he had no real right to do--to the Slovakians. It was only a few years ago that Slovakia and Czechoslovakia became independent countries again.

***

So, that is how Josef Hoffman and his friends got their names onto a political dissident list when Eddy was a young boy. Luckily, Josef was also friends with the local mayor and chief of police, both Christians and Carpathians. While he was intermittently a wanted fugitive, because he supported the socialists, he remained a respected member of the community.

***

According to family lore, Eddy's *grandfather* Adolf Frid (his mother's father) had been killed when a cannonball hit him while he was eating in camp, during a battle with the Russians in WWI. He had fought many glorious battles, barely surviving numerous hand-to-hand clashes, survived by the narrowest of margins, smaller than the edge of a bayonet, but his end came with the bluntness of a cannon ball, shot blindly from afar while he perhaps ate his military rations.

In 1938 Eddy's father was drafted into the Czech Calvary. The Czech's were laying claim to Solazia, a land on the northern border of Czechoslovakia, still technically in Poland.

***

as told to Gordon Richiusa

Eddy's mother had developed a hatred and fear of the Germans (1942) because, at one point, when the German controlled military were trying to locate Eddy's father, they detained her for *questioning*.

In 1936 Ed's father had been in a Czechoslovakian prison for about six months, because he was the head of the Communist party. When Eddy's father was a fugitive, they arrested Eddy's mother to interrogate her as to the whereabouts of her husband. She was beaten and tortured for days before being released, pleading the entire time ignorance of her husband's whereabouts or political leanings.

***

In his early years, from what Eddy could remember, his life was very good; the family business was successful and his father was a local leader in the community. The entire Village sported the family name.

Then, sometime prior to Eddy's bar mitzvah, Eddy's father disappeared again. Just prior to this, Eddy had been attending daily Hebrew studies classes. A rabbi was conducting classes and accepted Eddy to the group close by, because of the proximity to the town and school.

Eddy found the rabbi to be a little too strict and willing to use a long whip-like switch to strike students even in the furthest seats away from the front of the class for giving wrong answers to his questions.

One day, Eddy was sitting next to a much smaller friend who was the recipient of several of these strikes. The rabbi seemed to be targeting this one classmate on this particular day to the point of causing his friend to become completely terrified. His fear caused him to be unable to answer the most simple question.

"Do you even know your name?"

"Uh, huh, I..."

With remarkable accuracy that must have been born from practice, the rabbi's switch came down between the other students and desks landing once again on the bare hand of Eddy's hapless friend.

An overdeveloped sense of justice welled up inside of Eddy, and he instantly jumped from his seat, charging the rabbi.

He grabbed the rabbi by the beard and and pushed him up against the blackboard at the front of class.

"Don't do that again," Eddy said simply while the rabbi looked understandably both shocked and angered that his authority had been questioned.

Before the rabbi could respond, Eddy ran out of the classroom and straight to his house to find his father and confess. Unfortunately there was no one home. So Eddy locked the door and waited silently inside.

Minutes later the rabbi came to the house and started knocking loudly. He didn't seem particularly angry or out of control, as Eddy expected. The knocking continued for a couple of minutes and finally stopped as abruptly as it began

"What is it Bumi? Why are you standing there?" his father asked when he came home and found Eddy standing patiently in the center of the living room.

"I wanted to be the first to tell you. I grabbed the rabbi by the beard and pushed him against the classroom wall."

"Why would you do such a thing?"

"He was hitting my friend with his whip."

"Your friend? What did your friend do?"

"Nothing. The rabbi uses his switch every class time."

"Has he ever hit you?"

"No."

"So what happened?

Eddy went on to recreate the incident for his father.

"So, you were protecting your friend?"

"Yes sir."

"I probably would have done the same thing," his father added.

Eddy was forced to continue his religious training with another rabbi much further away from town until the time he had his bar mitzvah. This ceremony was strictly for the young men, as young girls did not receive the same training until this practice was introduced in the United States much later.

***

During this significant religious-training period, there was another incident that helped define for Eddy not only a moral standard, but allowed him to see his father in a realistic light. Eddy's father was not really devout, but wanted to make his wife and his father happy, so he allowed them to plan Bumi's Bar Mitzvah.

Eddy's options for religious training were now very limited, since the incident with the rabbi was not the first time that Bumi had lost his temper in a classroom. On another day, on the way to school Eddy and his friend Ernie got into an argument.

Eddy and Ernie were not great friends, but Eddy kept his cool. Later the boys arrived to the classroom and a smaller boy who had traditionally been seated next to Eddy near a window was being targeted by Ernie. Perhaps Ernie took Eddy's ignoring of being kicked as a sign of weakness, or maybe it caused Ernie to continue his bullying.

Even though Eddy did not know the smaller boy's name, when the smaller boy started to cry, Eddy simply lost control.

He got up from his seat and without conversation, picked the older boy up like a bar-bell, holding him parallel to the ground, over his head and threw him over the second story ramp where they were standing. Ernie tumbled onto the ground landing on a metal shoe scrapper and ripped open his chin.

Almost immediately, Eddy knew he had made a serious mistake. There was a dull thud from below and the sounds of loud moaning, so he knew at least that Ernie was still alive. Eddy did not bother to look out of the window, but ran, along with the smaller boy and several others who had just witnessed Eddy's protective outburst out the door, down the hall and down the stairs through the doorway which led to the courtyard where the young Ernie lay writhing and clutching alternately his right leg, shoulder, and chin. Eddy ran to get a doctor, but did not return with him to see what happened to Ernie.

Later that day, the younger boy came to Eddy's home and told him that Ernie had broken a leg and cracked a few ribs, as well as a badly cut chin and other bruises and bumps that would take a month or two to fully heal, Ernie considered himself lucky.

Eddy felt horrible and considered himself extremely lucky. He vowed to control his anger and blinding sense of morals from then onward. Ernie and Eddy remained distant friends with Ernie totally getting out of the bully business.

***

Eddy's father just before leaving to become a member of the rebel forces said, "Bumi, keep an eye on your mother. I'll keep in touch with you if I can. You are the oldest and you need to take care of the family." With this, Eddy's father took some cash from his pocket and tried to hand it to Eddy.

"Thanks, but I don't need it," Bumi told his father.

"Oh?"

And, Eddy told his father of his daily enterprises and pulled his own wad of cash from his pocket.

His father's eye glistened with pride, but his admiration and love went unspoken. Both simply put their money back into their own pockets. They knew that Bumi would take care of the family while Josef was away.

With that his father went into hiding. Eddy was now the head of the house. With Eddy's mother and two siblings to support, he made the decision to travel 250 miles away to Budapest in search of work.

When he got to Budapest, Eddy's first job was an apprentice in a machine shop. He had to do a lot of heavy lifting of supplies and machinery. The lifting was hard but he did the best that a child could do. After a few months, he switched jobs for better pay with Lampart Cailard-Uzle, an exclusive crystal chandelier company on Erzsebet Street Circle.

Eddy's responsibility was to help the electrician with assembly, delivery and installation. On the side, to make more money, he made a deal with the electrician and started making appointments with the customers for evening and weekend installations. The electrician paid Eddy a fee and he would get tips from the other customers as well. It was good money and Eddy was able to send it home to support the family.

Unfortunately, the lifting he had done the year before caused a hernia and he had to have an operation in Budapest. While he was recuperating in the hospital, Eddy had a visit from a Jewish couple that owned the largest bitters factory in Budapest. They were looking to adopt a boy and they chose Eddy. He told them no, that he had his own family. That is when he decided he had to return home.

as told to Gordon Richiusa

When he got home sometime in late January or early February from Budapest, within a couple of days of arriving it was clear that things had changed. It was made known that everyone had been ordered to wear the star of David on their clothing. And, if that wasn't bad enough, every Jew had to make their own star. It was the law, everywhere. Ed didn't know it at the time, but his village was not the only one that was being treated like farm animals.

***

It 1943 the atrocities planned for the Jews were an extremely well kept secret. No one outside of the Nazi hierarchy, knew that anything was going on. There was no communication. They simply had no idea. When the Germans told everyone that they needed help in factories. No one fought. No one suspected.

It was about 7A.M. in the morning. The first house they hit was the Hoffman house. Eddy and his friends were sweeping the streets. They noticed the night before that some of the Hungarian military went up to some of the homes with machine guns. It wasn't aggressive. They were just putting everybody's name on a list. The Germans and local police were always making lists of something.

The Nazis, in support of the Hungarians, put up ugly looking fencing around these blocks to keep the Jews in, saying at first it was for their own protection. This was called the Ghetto.

Ode to Life!

When the soldiers came to Bumi's house, his family took a few personal items and some food, locked the door, not knowing when they'd see their home again, (but thinking that they would be back) and left.

When they went to each family's door, the Nazis checked off names from the list they made the morning before. No one asked about Eddy's father, Josef having already known that he was in hiding.

There were regular homes and apartments in the ghetto. It was about a mile square. There were thousands of people in the ghetto. It was late winter. Eddy, his family and all the others rounded up from the town were there about two and a half months.

***

Eddy's Grandfather's house was inside the chain link fencing. Eddy and his family stayed in the attic. A typical day was spent watching his mother cook breakfast and lunch. The family had dug a hole in the basement, put food in with straw on top and covered it with dirt. They had a certain amount of vegetables. Eddy's mother would ration out some of the food from the hole, but there was less and less food because there was never much given to the families. Other families did the same thing.

There was no sense of urgency. Everyone was just waiting things out. After all, the rabbis were mostly making the point that apart from appearances, everyone was still alive and safe. So, they waited. Eddy played cards with his friends during the day. The Jews didn't rise up against the

Germans in the Ghetto. The rabbis said, "Look, we are honest people; we are not harming anybody. Some of us are old; some are very young. We're of no use to them. Why should the Germans hurt us?"

Jewish stores were allowed to operate as usual for the first few days. But, once everyone was in the Ghetto, permission to leave was suddenly revoked and all normal work stopped. Now it was too late.

The Ghetto was surrounded by guards. No one was leaving. There were no supplies coming in. Rationing was a part of life, only a small amount of bread a day, less than a half of pound of bread for his family.

It was 1942, and the head of the Hoffman household, Bumi Hoffman was just thirteen years of age.

Eddy always felt a little like a failure for not being able to fulfill his promise to his father.

Those who were able went to the rabbis and other elders with their concerns. Still, the rabbis were perplexed, *"Why would they want to hurt us? It doesn't make sense."* The rabbis said.

No one in Eddy's family or any of the others rose up against the soldiers in the Ghetto. The rabbis perhaps were just trying to make people feel better, but looking back Eddy could not believe that it was so easy for the Nazis.

***

Then it happened. Eddy and his entire family were marched straight to the railroad station.

"Take only what you can easily carry, nothing extra. Hurry, Hurry! We must leave now!"

Without warning, the familiar Hungarian soldiers appeared and everyone was herded toward the train station. Eddy thought that he recognized some of them from his enterprise of selling candy and cards.

Walking into the open for the first time in months, Eddy could see all the people in the Ghetto were being escorted into lines and marched onto trains in dozens of cattle cars. The trains were stacked up end to end, and stretched far into the distance. The soldiers put 75 people in a cattle car. Hungarian and Russian townspeople, not Jews lined the streets and train station, many smiling and laughing.

The train was very large. That's all Eddy could ascertain, but Eddy couldn't count them, as he was making sure his family was being placed together. He had promised his father he would take care of the family.

Eddy's grandfather, uncle, his brothers, his mother and his cousins were all in one cattle car together, standing, because there was no room to sit. Before entering, Eddy had seen that soldiers sat atop the cars, not inside, and watched silently, without expression.

The doors were suddenly shut, and there was only half a window with bars on the upper side of the car for air. The train started and moved at a moderate pace for maybe three or four hours. Then moving over for another train at a station with extra tracks, there might be a short slowdown or pause. It was hard to tell time because there was only that one small window near the roof of the car, where the Hungarian soldiers could sometimes be heard walking on top of the car.

Eddy's grandfather was 92 years old so he was allowed to squeeze the younger family members together so at least they would have enough room to sit and be able to sleep.

Some of the women had taken a little food and water and covered it up in the corner of the cattle-car. There was a small hole in the floor where people had to maneuver for relieving themselves. It was inadequate for the job, and by the smell it was obvious that most did not bother to aim carefully after the first day.

The horrible smell of human waste was almost overwhelming. Time moved very slowly. The train kept moving.

On the second day of travel, in the middle of the night, Eddy's mother tried to hang herself.

Eddy was wedged into a corner near his grandfather and was trying to sleep. Eddy did not know what had happened, but awoke to hear his uncle's voice, "Hold her up! Hold her up. Untie her. Let her down!"

This was followed by the sobs of his mother, begging to be allowed to die.

She must have had help tying a scarf through the bars of the only window near the ceiling of the car.

Eddy's uncle had saved his mother's life, but she was half gone. While others showed sadness and concern, Eddy was mad about what his mother had done because he

Ode to Life!

thought, "How dare my mother do that? How could she think about leaving me and my brothers?"

He was resentful. He was a kid. He did not understand.

***

The last time Eddy saw his father was the beginning of 1943, just before they were moved into the ghetto. Josef Hoffman left to fight with the resistance in the mountains. Eddy didn't know what happened to his father throughout the war. He found out afterward when he had come back from the camps that his father had been killed. He never did find out any details, and no family stories were ever told, as was the case with his grandfather. What Eddy did learn was that Josef was fighting with the Partisans (Russian Communists) against the Germans and he was shot. Eddy didn't know where, when, or how this happened and it didn't matter.

What Eddy didn't know was that his mother had been tortured by the police and soldiers when they first started looking for Ed's father who had disappeared.

***

Suddenly, the train switched tracks and headed toward Czechoslovakia instead of going toward Hungary. This was suspicious to Eddy and many others. Some called out from car to car, but whispered protests and general confusion were mainly the results.

"What's happening?" Some called to the soldiers, but there was no response and still no way of knowing what horrors lay ahead.

as told to Gordon Richiusa

Then, another curious thing occurred. The train stopped perhaps in a depot or maybe in the middle of nowhere. Eddy could not tell.

Someone in the next car must have pulled themselves up to the tiny window to observe the activity going on outside. Voices called from one car to the next. Everyone went silent and then it was confirmed that the Hungarian military were jumping off the train and the German military were jumping on.

Eddy thought at first perhaps this meant that they were going to inland Hungary to work at *factories,* as had been the rumor. Instead they took a right turn when the guards were changed and started heading straight toward Germany. This first train trip took about 2 ½ days.

Since everyone was potentially set for extermination, no one in the trains were offered water or food. There was only that one small window high above everyone's head. It was an ordeal to shift around and get a chance to peek out. So, only a few took on this responsibility at this point. To add to the horror, it was just too small to squeeze through, even for the smallest, skinniest person such as Eddy.

Although no one in Eddy's car had died yet, everyone was grumpy, but still standing strong in most cases. Eddy decided that he would never give up like his mother did. That was the common attitude; *no matter what happens, never give up*.

After all, Eddy had his dream to comfort him, but not much else. Things may have started to look desperate, but at the same time Eddy had a strong belief that he would survive anything. He was sad however that his dream didn't show the same for any of his friends or other members of his family.

as told to Gordon Richiusa

Chapter Three
Winners and Losers

It was after WWII had ended, with the liberation of Eddy from Ebensee, that Eveline met, fell in love with and married Eddy Hoffman. In later years Eddy had said it was love at first sight for him. He also joked that he, an American citizen had married a foreigner--like all jokes, there was a thread of truth to this--but Eveline also knew she should take Eddy's every statement with a grain of salt. Eddy had become a citizen because he was drafted into the U.S. Military shortly after arrival in the U.S. There was a program for immigrants in place at the time that allowed a fast-track to citizenship for honorable service. Eddy had taken advantage of this offer and was a citizen when the two had met.

Eveline had also always acknowledged that, at their first meeting she was immediately impressed with the dashing style of her blind date. On the ride home from the **Children of the Shoah** meeting, Eveline had let her mind wander to a photograph that Eddy had in his wallet which was taken of himself and a friend who did not even know that Eveline existed. When tracking the arc of time that brought these two together, a fairytale kind of Fate often seemed to play a hand in their coming together, their union, and the unfolding of events like the one at the meeting.

Ode to Life!

For the days that followed the sudden-trauma event, Eveline's mind continued to find itself immersed in the past. After her parents had been allowed to immigrate to the U.S. to retrieve their children in 1948, the family was moved back to France, partly because Simon wanted to recapture the family's lost lives and partly because their permission to stay in America was not permanent, as yet. Simon didn't want to give up being French. He and Anna had made the very difficult decision to separate their entire family for a long period of time in dedication to what he felt were French ideals. The truth was that if Anna and Simon had NOT done what they did, there was a very high likelihood that none of the Grossmans would have survived, since girls and many of the women were summarily executed upon arrival in the camps.

***

Anna and Simon too were experiencing trauma, no doubt and it was always silently agreed that the phrase "you can't go home again" made popular by Thomas Wolfe could have been used to describe this brief period of Eveline's family's life. Many great sages express that the common source of dissatisfaction for people is an inability to live in the present. Problems only really destroy the lives of those who live in the past or the future. For whatever reason, Simon was not as Eveline had idealized him to be. He was often angry, and the girls had grown into young, Americanized women.

as told to Gordon Richiusa

Eveline had spoken and written about her experiences in hiding, but "like an outsider looking in" feeling almost like these were made up myths. She was proud of her French heritage, but felt that she was 100% American, since she had moved to USA in 1943, and though she had reluctantly returned to Paris briefly, she had spent by that time most of her life in the United States.

And the reality was that even before the war, Simon was a hard one to deal with. One memory Eveline had was of Paulette breaking the very important short-wave radio that belonged to Simon. Of course Eveline was the instigator, as she had goaded the young Paulette, barely 3 years old to find out *where the voice was coming from inside the little box* that her father had warned of never coming near.

The source of the voice was not found, but the short wave radio, a collection of fragile tubes and wires ended up broken. Since short wave radios were a prize possession, in high demand, when Simon came home and found out what had happened, he flew into a rage.

Almost as if it had been pre-planned, both girls were immediately taken outside to face one of their greatest fears...the family rooster. Although Eveline struggled, Simon took the girls forcedly outside, turned Paulette over his knee, putting corn on her behind and let the rooster peck the corn from her bare bottom forcing Eveline to watch. The terror that already existed welled inside Eveline because she knew that her turn was coming. He repeated this punishment with Eveline.

This type of behavior was often repeated by Simon. Many years later, when the family had returned to Paris, a teenaged Eveline was trying to exercise her independence. She could not remember the exact details of the incident, but Simon was so enraged that he forced Eveline to submit to his authority by commanding her to kneel down and kiss her father's feet. Eveline, in a dangerous act of rebellion, slyly put her hand in front of her mouth in such a way as to hide it from Simon. She kissed her own hand, but prevented any further punishment.

Ironically, it was Eveline's job to keep her father's shoes clean. He would place his shoes outside his bedroom, in a row, once a week, and it was expected that Eveline would shine and polish all of them. They were probably clean enough to kiss without concern.

All three girls had grown very independent by this time, especially Jackie who was the oldest and had been forced to mature more quickly than her two siblings. They had all grown up, to a great degree in America. This meant that their standards for how young women should be treated were much different than old world Europe. However, Simon Le Terreur longed for the family life that he felt was stolen from him by the nazis.

So, in 1952, after the constant complaining of his daughters, Eveline and Paulette, Simon gave in and brought the family back to the U.S.

Anna had easily adapted the American ways and values with those of her homeland. Making matches for her girls, therefore was simply something that mothers did around the world. In that context, Eveline and Eddy met and their match was a by-product of a plot that Anna had hatched.

The opportunity for family intrigue had just arrived from Paris. Anna made friends easily. One of these new American friends was a woman named Suzanne, who had a brother named Roger. The connect was that Suzanne and Roger were also from Paris and Eveline and her sisters still considered themselves part French. Roger had also been introduced to Eddy Hoffman, a few times as they were all associating with the same survivor community. Eddy was living with his 1st cousin Joe Hoffman and Joe's wife Ruth.

None of the youngsters knew that they were being set up, except perhaps Roger, who may have asked for help getting a blind date with a young girl named Paulette. Here was the matchmaker's plot: A friend of Anna, named Suzanne casually brought up the subject.

Roger (Suzanne's brother) had been living in Paris and Suzanne had decided to introduce him to the two eligible sisters because Paulette and Eveline had a similar background as Roger. They were all from France and they were Jewish.

Suzanne (Mrs. Schmoock) was close to Anna's age. Eddy and Eveline paid no attention to one another. Indeed, one did not know that the other existed.

All of the young people who had come from foster care or orphanages had stayed friendly when they met again in the U.S., but Eveline and Eddy were unknown to each other at the time. Suzanne knew of Eddy as she was close to Eddy's cousin Perry, as did her husband who was from a town near where Eddy lived in Europe. Roger was one of the young people who met Eddy through his sister.

Earlier, Eddy had asked about the unusual spelling of Suzanne and Roger's last name. Suzanne told Eddy she had changed her name.

"Why?" he asked.

"How would you like to be known as Mrs. Schmuk?" she asked. No more was said on the subject.

Later, when Anna suggested that the girls go on a double date, as far as Eveline was concerned, she and her younger sister were being given a green light for a night out with a guy who spoke French and another person who had a car. The proposition had the makings of a wonderful night on the town for them.

***

"Wouldn't it be great if we could match my brother with one of your daughters?" Suzanne had asked Anna earlier, not caring anything about the second person (Eddy). Roger had said that Eddy was his first choice for such a date, because he knew that Eddy owned a vehicle.

Suzanne knew that "*he was quite popular with the ladies and a confirmed bachelor.*" It didn't matter much, since this was only going to be one date.

Paulette on the other hand just liked the idea of dating as it was fairly new to her. She was very beautiful and was often the focus of interest for other young men her age.

When the proposition of the blind date was presented to the sisters, only Roger's cultural background was given as the reason for the support by Anna and Suzanne, "He's French and you are French," they said.

Eveline was not too happy about going on a blind date with just anyone, but the girls were excited about going out together and a night on the town was the gold standard of dating in those days. Also, it was a little lonely on the West Side of Cleveland where the girls now resided, and their experiences in foster care had apparently strengthened their already tight bonds.

"If Paulette wants to go, she can have Roger," Eveline had said, thinking she was being generous. "I will take the other one."

Eddy had already gotten enough information about the two sisters to realize that he would be with Eveline. "I'm older than everyone," he thought. "And, since one is older than the other, I'll take the older one."

There was only one double-edged catch. Eddy didn't want to break two dates that he already had on the weekend in question. It was an hour's drive to the Grossmans.

Roger met with and begged Eddy one final time. "Please, Eddy! I really would like to go out with this girl, but you know how women are. She won't go out with me unless someone takes out her sister, Eveline."

Ode to Life!

Roger was getting desperate and embellished, "She won't go on a blind date with *anyone* except you. I don't know what you've got, probably the new car".

"If you can't find someone else, there must be a reason," Eddy said.

"That's the reason! She won't go unless YOU go. And the sisters stick together. You've got the Pontiac! It will be fun and I NEED you."

"Fine. I'll be your chauffeur, but just this one date and if it starts to go badly, I'm going home early."

It took some tap-dancing, but Eddy was used to making excuses for cancelling dates. He was already worried about the dilemma he was facing with two dates on the same night, anyway. This way he could get out of both previous dates, and blame his good nature for wanting to help out a friend.

On the night of the date, Eddy and Roger showed up to pick up the girls. Eddy's new Pontiac was the envy all his friends and most who did not even know who Eddy was as well.

Eddy took one look at Eveline and felt as though he was struck by a bolt of lightening. He was glad that he'd said he would take the older girl, and there was something else. He had a feeling that he knew Eveline's face very well, like it was very familiar. That's because it was familiar.

Before Eddy and Eveline had met "officially" Eddy's friend who had been in the military with him, a guy named

Art had gone to a Cleveland Heights Temple where the young Jews gathered for some dancing and fun.

There were around seventy or eighty young people who had gathered frequently because they felt the common bond of surviving the Nazis. They were all International Students mixed culturally to some degree, but mostly Holocaust survivors themselves.

"Hey, Eddy. Take a picture with me, " Art had said when Eddy came into the dance hall. Eddy stood next to his friend with dozens of others in the background. A few days later, they gave the developed picture to Eddy. That photo was taken months prior to the first date, and Eddy had paid no attention to the background of the photograph that he was given by the person who had taken the picture. He had merely folded the edges just enough as to make it fit snuggly into his wallet and forgotten about it.

***

Eddy had paid cash for the car with money he had earned in the military and from an assembly line cake baker job he'd taken immediately upon returning to the U.S. after service. Eddy always managed to have money. After all, he was a survivor.

"What happened?" Roger asked. "I thought this car was a lemon that wouldn't go more than 18 miles per hour."

"I had to take it in to get it fixed," Eddy relayed. He had an ongoing problem because the mechanics found small pieces of metal in the gearbox. After cleaning out, the lemon became, not a peach, but at least an orange...only half sour in Eddy's words.

When the door was opened, Simon and Anna answered.

They liked Roger because he was a Jewish French Boy, but they needed to size up Eddy as a matter of protocol.

"Would you like a drink?" Simon asked.

Eddy, "No thank you."

"What kind of a man are you?" Simon Le Terreur snapped. "You don't drink?"

In a Jewish family, when someone comes over you offer them a little Schnapps, it's customary. Criticizing how they respond to the offer is what made Simon "the Terreur."

Anna gave Simon a tilt of her head which Eveline had come to know meant she was displeased, Mr. Grossman anxiously began a series of questions:

"Where are you from? What do you do for a living? How long have you been here? Do you have relatives here?" And so on.

Eddy spoke sparingly but honestly, and told him he had been in Auschwitz and could speak a little Polish and Yiddish. He then spoke in Polish to Simon at that moment, which seemed to seal the deal for the night. Despite this, Eveline's parents never really took to Eddy, because they felt he was too quiet.

Then, the sisters made their entrance. When Eveline appeared, Eddy knew the meaning of **love at first sight,** but also felt that he had seen Eveline somewhere before.

He didn't realize that he was carrying at that moment the photograph with the folded sides in his wallet of Eveline's smiling face. In the photo Eveline was in the background, seated at a table in the back of the dining hall. Now, meeting Eveline officially for the first time Eddy felt an unusual sense of recognition. Eveline looked familiar and Eddy didn't know why. Anna made the formal introductions. "This is Paulette," She said speaking mostly to Roger. "And, this is Eveline."

Eveline had set her eyes on Eddy and her first thought was a pedestrian one, "W*hat a nice suit. Navy blue."*

She had no way of knowing that Eddy didn't have many clothes when he got to America, just one small suitcase. He had obtained the suit for his many escapades with the ladies."

Eveline and Paulette were escorted outside and into the Pontiac. Eveline thought, "Nice blue car. He is very quiet though." Then she asked, "Do you smoke?"

"No, I hate smoking."

Well, I can't tell him that I smoke. "I don't smoke either, " she said.

Paulette did NOT like Roger. He tried to put his hands all over her and Eveline could hear from the backseat, *"Well, you're French aren't you?"*

***

They couples drove to Akron and went dancing.

Aside from Paulette being exhausted from wrestling in the back seat with Roger, both pairs parted friends.

The next day, Eddy called for the second date. Eveline was waiting for that call and was very excited but she let Paulette answer the phone and they pretended that Eveline had to be found. After making Eddy wait for a short time, Eveline said yes.

The second date did not have another couple to interfere and Eddy took Eveline dancing again.

Still, there was no kiss.

***

Before the third date Paulette called Eddy to see if he was really interested. Eveline had put her sister up to the call. She wanted to make sure Eddy was kept interested and thought that this was a good way to do it.

Paulette looked for a different kind of guy than Eveline. She liked the more fun types. Eveline looked for good character, qualities that she thought would be attractive over the long haul, at least more than just a date night or two.

At the time of this date, Jacqueline was already married to Alan--her high school sweetheart. Alan was in medical school. They had a small apartment with a refrigerator that had a coil at the top. Jackie didn't like Eddy too much because he was so quiet and she wasn't certain that he had anything "upstairs."

***

On the third date, the couple went for a ride to a Park in Lakewood.

Eveline was very nervous, Ed was showing signs of seriousness and making some moves that, although expected still made Eveline concerned. She noticed her mouth was extremely dry.

"I'm really thirsty," she said simply.

"I know where you can get some water," Eddy said and minutes later he pulled through the gates of a park and along side a water fountain.

"Here it is," Eddy proclaimed like he was discovering the Fountain of Youth and turned off the car.

"You don't need to shut off the car, " she said. She was worried that if the car was off that they were technically "parking" and everyone knew what that would lead to.

"But, I'm thirsty too." Eddy said. "I need to get some water."

Eveline moved fast from the car and got her drink, keeping the length of parking time to a minimum. Eddy followed behind Eveline and put his hand on the fountain and took a sip.

"Let's go!" Eveline said, before Eddy could wipe his mouth, and the pair went dancing at another local club. Eveline was impressed by Eddy's worldly knowledge. He seemed to know all the fun and practical places.

***

After the date Eddy drove straight to Eveline's home and approaching the door, on the porch steps Eddy kissed Eveline for the first time. She thought, "What a great kisser! He must be very experienced."

It was a nice long kiss, both respectful and full of passion. Then, before it could get awkward Eddy backed off and gently turned Eveline toward the door.

In later years the two versions of what happened next were slightly different. Both Eddy and Eveline agreed that at this moment, Eveline stumbled slightly and Ed had to place both hands around her waist to keep her steady. She told Eddy that it was the stairs that had caused her to misstep, but he said that she was merely swooning because of the kiss.

Eveline wanted to go to a University, but being a girl her parents did not see the value. Why should they send her to college when she was just going to get married and waste the education anyway. When Eveline had enrolled into a secretarial course--her parents did not want to pay for her to go to college or secretarial school; so Eveline put herself through school and earned a certificate. She stayed at her family home while doing this.

She had plans though, she wanted to move to Greenwich Village in New York and live the exciting life of being single there with her French cousin Michele. She could hardly wait.

For some reason she was worried about her father. She knew that Simon being of old-fashioned, European stock would not care for any suitor unless marriage was the end goal. A few months later Ed was already talking about marriage.

Simon was cautious. So, as soon as the subject was brought up by Eddy, Eveline shared this information with her parents. To Eveline's surprise, Anna was more cautious than Simon, but Simon put one condition on this talk of marriage, "I won't believe anything until he gives you a ring."

Some of Eddy's friends had made a good living in the jewelry business and Eddy ordered a modest ring through them and gave it to Eveline. At this point Paulette decided that she wanted to make it a double wedding. So, Anna and Simon went through the motions planning a big double wedding, because Simon didn't want to plan two single weddings one after another. However they still hoped that Eveline would change her mind. Also, Eveline did not think that Paulette was ready for marriage, and was only thinking about it because she didn't want to stay home with Simon and Anna.

Eveline's parents were still not fans of Eddy, and in one last effort to scratch the whole thing, they offered to pay for a one way trip to California to get Eveline far away from her fiancée.

Jacqueline and Alan were out in San Francisco and this would give Eveline a place to live while she sorted out her feelings. Alan was an intern in the Navy.

Ode to Life!

Eveline and Eddy had already decided that they would have a June wedding. The details would be locked down in the near future. Eveline was having to deal with her parents constantly trying to destroy the relationship. At the time, Eddy was 27. He didn't feel that he had to discuss anything with Eveline's parents, Eveline was 19.

Eveline was feeling overwhelmed and without discussing it with Eddy, she took her father's offer and with only a one-way ticket went to California. In her head, she was not saying goodbye but merely exerting her autonomy. As soon as she arrived in San Francisco, she wrote Eddy to let him know where she was, that it was not a goodbye letter, but a plea for a little space to think about her future.

Eddy and Eveline saved many of their letters. Here is what transpired over the course of a two week period. Eveline's sister was also not happy with Eveline's choice for a future husband, so she and Alan encouraged Eveline to settle into San Francisco life, asking her to go to a party with them because there would be some other doctors there. Jackie wanted her sister to perhaps meet someone, maybe a doctor, as she had and take her mind off of Eddy.

She had not spoken to Eddy prior to her leaving, and as soon as she landed in California, she penned the following letter:

My Darling Eddy,
I'm in San Francisco. My sister Jackie invited me to stay with her while I took

some time and clear my head from the negative influence and constant bickering from my parents. They, as you know have been trying to manipulate me to not go ahead with our engagement.

Coming here is a decision I made on my own, and I am hoping you understand that I also do not want to feel as though I'm being pressured by anyone, including you.

Again, I hope you understand.

I love you, Eveline

This letter was received by Eddy on a Saturday. He lived with his cousin Andrew, with Andrew's wife Perry and their three boys in their large house in Cleveland. Eddy's feelings were hurt when he received Eveline's letter, especially since she did not discuss the trip with him prior to leaving. Sometimes people just have to be alone. Eveline just needed some alone time to clear her head. Also, Eddy had one of his many migraine headaches. This is the letter he wrote when he received the Dear Eddy Letter (as he called it later) from his fiancée:

My Darling Eveline,

I'm sorry you feel that way. I feel that we are engaged and you should sort out *your feelings and return to Cleveland by Thursday, or our engagement is off.*

Your loving fiancée,
Eddy

Before the day of his ultimatum, Eveline received a second letter from Ed.

My Darling Eveline,

First I am sorry about the last letter I wrote you, and besides I had a headache. You forgive me and Eveline, I'm writing to you with a pencil because I could not find a pen. It's about 11:30 P.M. and I'm in bed. I will send this letter tomorrow when I go to work, so you will be able to get it Tuesday. I miss you honey and I love you. What's the latest over there with your parents? I am angry with them. Well, you can't change them. That's how they are and Eveline, try not to argue with them too much. At the end everything will work out all right.

As you know, I'm moving this week and it will take a bit of doing with all my junk and papers. Write me when you are coming, so that I should expect you and what time, not like the last time. Today, I was working until 8:30 p.m. and then I went over to Bella's house to watch television. But, I came home 11 p.m. because I was planning to write you tonight, yet.

So, how are you? And, are you working this week? And, where have you been this weekend? What are you doing at nights?

I close now and I love you. Yours always.

Love Eddy xxxxxxxxxxxxxxxxxxxxx
P.S.
Did you hear anything from San Francisco? Are they alright?

Eveline did not take well to the ultimatum and called Eddy, who suggested that Eveline not call anymore because it was too expensive.

Shortly thereafter, Eveline returned to Cleveland and stayed with one of Eddy's cousins. From there she sent the following to her parents:

February 25, 1957
Dear Mom and Dad,

Well, this is it. I've made up my mind, and nothing in the world is going to change it. I've had ample time to think without interference, and I know what I want. And, what I want is the following. I know Paulette wants it too.

1) I love Eddy and I'm going to marry him. That's final.

2) The wedding will be a simple buffet after the ceremony, absolutely no dinner.

3) The fellas will invite as many people as they want.

4) They will pay only for the flowers, hats, and photographer's fee.

5) You pay for the wedding dresses and accessories. I realize now that the wedding has had much to do with my state of mind. It is only right that we get married the way we want, and if you do not agree Eddy and I will just elope.

No "ifs" or "buts." This is my wedding. I want to enjoy it. If Paulette still wants that big brawl you wanted, you can discuss that with her. I will have no part of it!

I will stay here until I get an answer one way or the other. If you decide to give us the kind of wedding we want, I want you to make all the arrangements with the caterer and Paulette, and give me proof that it has all been taken care of before I will consider coming back.

If I don't get an answer by next Monday (March 4th) I will assume your answer to be no to the five points I made in this letter.

Don't think you are going to change any of my ideas. I have never been more sure of anything in my life.

Love,
Evie

Simon and Anna surrendered silently, without anymore of a fight or even an acknowledgement. The wedding took place as Eveline and Eddy wanted. It was a double wedding with Paulette and Eddie Schlechter.

Of the 100 guests, most were invited by Eddy. About 20 were from the rest of the family.

Ode to Life!

as told to Gordon Richiusa

Chapter Four
Illuminating Darkness

"Everyone OUT! Hurry! Hurry! Hurry!"
"Jeder RAUS! Eile! Eile! Eile!"

When the train got to Auschwitz Eddy heard the same phrase repeated again and again, "Everyone out! Women on one side, men on the other. Hurry, hurry, hurry." This three stanza chant seemed to energize the prisoners. Prisoners on the platform whispered quietly to the new-comers, "Tell the Germans your child is a twin; they do not kill twins. They think they're special."

It was hard to know what to believe. Most did not take this seriously.

Eddys ninety two year old grandfather jumped out of the train like a young man. Believing that he was still in charge, he told Eddy's younger brother, "*Tibbi, you hold onto your mother.*"

The German's said in comforting voices, "Don't worry, you will find everyone later on."

Eddy decided that his grandfather was probably right and spoke hurriedly to his little brother, "Tibbi, You go with mother," Eddy hugged him before he walked away with her. Eddy's mother looked drawn and defeated. She took Tibbi's hand as a matter of motherly instinct. Tibbi looked back at Eddy as the two moved in the opposite direction on the platform. Eddy, his grandfather, uncle, cousin and brother Karl were in a different line. That would be the last time Ed would see his mother and younger brother. Why was everyone being pushed and prodded? What was the urgency?

Jewish prisoners, evidenced by the Stars on the lapels appeared from somewhere and started cleaning up the train cars which were fouled by human waste and the stench of death. Was that why the train was so clean when it came and took his whole family?

Everyone was being herded into lines, five to a row. Eddy, his uncle, brother Karl, Grandfather, and his cousin-- five Hoffmans were in one line.

Slowly everyone was shuffled toward a little table with a couple of chairs. A man in uniform was sitting in the middle at a table with two other officers. There was a father with actual twin boys in front of them. The father and twins were from Eddy;s hometown. The father seemed very interested in Eddy's group. The man in uniform told the twins to go one way and the father the other way. He gave Eddy and Karl a going over with his eyes and then said while pointing at each individual, assigning a number, "1,2,3 this way. 1,2 that way."

Eddy's grandfather and cousin went one way. Ed went the other believing he would see them later. Everything was done very quickly. The Germans were relentless; no one was given time to think. They were told again and again. *"Keep moving! Keep moving!"* Eddy felt like he *had* to move.

Eddy came to a big barrack and there he saw a huge pile of eye-glasses, shoes, hair, clothes, huge piles, countless numbers. Everyone then was told to take their clothes off.

Like sheep the Germans sheered everyone of their hair. There was left only one thin stripe down the middle of the head, from back to front, which would make the prisoners obvious to the locals should anyone decide to escape and ditch the uniform. The Nazis then gave the naked Jews a prison uniform and a beret. This was the only change of clothes Ed would receive during his entire slavery.

The middle of the barrack was a square, an Adobe fireplace Eddy thought. As the prisoners were herded through the front door they saw the stark scene of bunk-bed after bed. There were three layers of bunks. Each bunk was assigned nine people the same way they were sorted at the train platform. "1,2,3,4,5,6,7,8,9," an officer pointed, counted and moved to the next bunk, leaving the nine assigned to figure out the logistics of sleeping arrangements. The bunks were made of flat plywood, no mattress and on each side wood was exposed, about five or six inches higher. The barracks was silent. The prisoners, as now Eddy knew he was one, did not make a sound as each person when counted moved into position, trying to figure out the best way to put nine people onto a single bunk.

When this was done, the SS officer walked out unceremoniously and another prisoner (the apparent Kapo or trustee) moved to block the door and with his actions began the process of establishing a hierarchy and a set of rules.

In the barracks prisoners were allowed to socialize as long as it was orderly. However, they could not leave the barracks unless told to do so.

***

"How old are you?" A question came from the next bunk. This was Eugene Spiegel, a boy of about the same age.

"Fourteen," Ed responded. "What's your name?"

"Hershi Spiegel."

Hershi had two uncles there sleeping in the same bunk. Over the course of the several days he told Ed his story. The uncles had owned a lumber yard in Muckacs, the eastern part of Czechoslovakia. They too had been sorted into Ghettoes and then suddenly, without warning the group they were with was herded onto the same train as Eddy and his family and brought to Auschwitz.

Both Eugene and Eddy shared quietly their observations. When they went to sleep the wood was like a wet sponge under them. It was always cold and damp in the barracks. Two blankets were distributed for all nine people on a single bunk. Quickly analyzing the situation Eddy found that if he was on the end he was cold. The blankets were not big enough for nine people, even when they pressed their bodies tightly together. There were no assigned sleeping areas, so Eddy always tried to get in or near the middle. He was small enough that he could get away with it. Both he and Eugene decided that it was one advantage to being among the youngest in the barracks.

When it was time to sleep Eddy took off the beret he'd been assigned as well as his shoes, which he was allowed to keep. Prisoners were allowed to carry their own shoes or belt, but anything of worth did not last long, as Eddy was soon to find out.

They asked everyone to put their shoes on the floor, not to wear them into the bed.

Not wanting to have his shoes stolen the first time he took them off, and because there was still this slight gesture of normal human civility (e.g. not wearing your shoes to bed) Eddy decided to put his shoes into his cap and sleep on them. A secondary reason for this habit was that Eddy learned quickly that tired muscles, especially neck muscles weren't a good match for the hard constantly wet wood beams that supported the plank wood mattress. He decided to use his shoes inside his hat as a leather-hard pillow.

Quickly all those who made it past the first day got into a very rigid routine of work and sleep, and not much else. There was only one meal given a day to break the monotony. At 4 o'clock the prisoners (now everyone realized that's what they were) were allowed to walk past a dirty pot and receive a little nourishment. At first it was a kind of gruel and a piece of bread. In a short time, the gruel was eliminated from the menu and a single loaf of bread needed to be divided between the nine people who were his bunkmates.

It took about 3-4 days before Eddy began to figure out that people were being killed.

Eddy arrived at this conclusion based upon a series of observations.

First, there were actual printed signs, in the German language, that encouraged work: ***Arbeit macht frei*--** Literally: work makes free, or *Work will set you free*. Eddy could see that the work was real, but had lost hope that there was any immediate possibility of freedom.

The crematorium had the incinerators burning day and night. Nothing specifically identified the crematorium. There was no signage in other words, but there was the unmistakable, continuous smell of roasting human flesh.

All the women that had a child with them when they arrived, Eddy found out later, were immediately killed when they left the train station. Very young and very old were also killed the same day. The Germans didn't want to bother separating the women from the small children who were clinging to them. The women, therefore were killed with their children either in their arms, holding hands, or draped around their mother's legs. Eddy's little brother Tibbi, Eddy's mother, and all old people along with Eddy's grandfather were gassed on day one. They were taken to "showers" but instead of getting a cleaning, they were killed.

as told to Gordon Richiusa

There were some prisoners who had been there for a while and seemed to know what was happening. One of them said to Eddy "See that smoke over there?" pointing at the smokestack of the crematorium. "Those are the ones who've been killed."

Eddy understood what the smoke represented, but he was still stunned. He could not talk, but still it was an effort as he tried not to show any emotion. As the days went on Eddy observed that now and then the soldiers would come into the barracks and pull people out. He heard bits and pieces of information over the course of the next several weeks. Apparently, they were first gassing them, and then burning the bodies. In some instances later, public hanging (for fright effect) preceded the crematorium.

However, no matter how fast they worked their evil, the Nazis could not kill everybody fast enough. The factories needed workers, but the trains kept coming. Eddy noticed that it wasn't just a few people who were disappearing, it was thousands and thousands of people, whole barracks at times. The flames burned continually. The trains were always coming and going. New, mostly healthy workers were delivered to replace those who had been slaughtered. Business is business and workers needed to be kept in good supply. Every now and then a soldier would interfere with the sorting, or one would come directly into the barracks and ask if anyone had a trade.

Eddy realized this might be his only opportunity to set himself apart, and decided to share his observations with

Ode to Life!

his brother, his uncle, and those who he'd gained a friendship, including Hershi and Hershi's uncle.

"Everyone knows that we are at a death camp. No one is talking about revolting. Everyone is being kept to themselves. Whatever the plan is, it looks like it will take time and that it has been thought out carefully."

"But, why? What's going on? Why are they doing this to us? What did we do to them? We're not the enemy." Eddy's brother and uncle asked. Eddy did not know the details, only the horrors of the basic plan. He knew he had to stand out in some way, but not so much as as to attract *unwanted* attention.

There was a heavy wire fence all around the compound where several nationalities and groups were being sorted out. On the other side of the camp from Eddy's barracks was the gypsy camp. They would put whole families together in the gypsy camp, old, young, women, men. A little further away from the men's compound where Eddy and his family were, was a women's camp. These were women who had been kept alive for other jobs only suited to women Eddy assumed. There were no children in this camp, only women, so Eddy did not have any hopes that both his mother and younger brother had survived.

One time, the guards asked Eddy to carry something into a women's camp. He did what he was asked and saw some of the women. They asked Eddy questions about their loved ones but he had no idea what to answer, even if he knew. It was thousands of people! How could he answer these questions?

To the right of the gypsy camp was the crematorium. You could see some of the flames coming up. Eddy kept remembering what the prisoner had said to him, "Those are the ones who have been killed"

"*Not me*," Eddy thought. "*I am going to get out! I will slip through the cracks and survive, just like in my dream.*"

***

Eddy's brother Karl was twelve. Eddy was fourteen now and was the older brother. He had to make Karl leave with him. Staying where they were would only end one way, with their death. Eddy knew by now that he had sent his other brother to his end by telling him to "Stay with mother." Either way, poor Tibbi did not fit the mold. He was too young to work and not close enough in age to his other brothers to pretend they were twins. Anyway, it was too late now. Staying alive another day was more pressing than past mistakes.

So Eddy said to his brother Karl, "Karl, next time they come around asking for trades people we are going to volunteer. You hear me? You are coming with me. You, me and Uncle are getting out of here, to where ever the Germans send us."

Eddy's uncle said, "No. I'm not going."

Karl decided to listen to his uncle instead of Bumi. They had been in Auschwitz for four weeks.

"You have to listen to me," Eddy said. "No one lives if they stay here."

But, Karl and Eddy's uncle would not listen.

"I'll volunteer too," said Hershi, his friend. This decision saved their lives.

***

Since there were so many crews coming and going, people did not always finish a day's work at the same time. No one was allowed to just sit in the barrack, however. Everyone either worked or stood as still as possible outside, in plain view of the guards. They had nothing and were given nothing extra. As a way of adding insult to injury, there was always the cold to contend with. People were pushed together into circles. No one had any clothing but a pajama. They worked and slept in the same clothes.

Eddy was impressed by the low clouds that hung over the entire camp most of the time. The stagnant mist that shrouded the air most of the time reminded him about his dream.

Everyday was dedicated to survival. Everyone could smell burning flesh constantly and the smell of burning bodies permeated every corner of the camp. He was growing desperate and knew it was only a matter of time before he and his other relatives would be killed.

A few days later Hershi confided to Eddy, "Two of my uncles are here with me, Sam and Adolf. My uncle Adolf has managed to bring some diamonds in."

"Diamonds?" Eddy asked, "Why?"

"You never know when you might have to pay off someone."

Adolf Spiegel, a very rich man before imprisonment had hidden several dozen diamonds in his anal cavity wrapped in a prophylactic. In later years Eddy wondered how many diamonds had been used to save Adolf Spiegel's, or some other poor Jews life, maybe even Eddy's.

***

There were two camps. Next to Auschwitz was Birkenau (a full-on extermination camp). Eddy and his family were in the extermination camp, Birkenau. Eddy didn't get a number tattooed. He had to memorize it. It was a simple method of keeping track of individuals. If someone tried to escape, the tattoo would make it obvious who they were and where they actually belonged. There were special markings in front or back of most numbers showing what ethnicity, or religion, or what crime they may have committed, or even political party you belonged to. Since Eddy volunteered to work in another labor camp they didn't tattoo him, because he left the camp before they had a chance. To this day, Eddy remembers his number as being: 42117.

***

The day after Eddy talked to his brother a couple of German officers came to the group and were looking for *facman* or trades people.

"If you have a trade, step out. We need you," they said.

So Eddy stepped out. To his brother he said in a rush, "Karl, let's go!"

"No, no," Karl said.

Eddy said, "I have to get out of here. They are going to kill everyone here. Please come. We have to get out."

Eddy's brother answered again, "No. I'm staying with my uncle."

Eddy and Karl's uncle, Simon was forty-three years old. Perhaps Karl thought Bumi was going crazy. Perhaps, to make himself feel better Eddy thought to himself, "*My uncle will keep an eye on Karl. He is an adult and I am not. They won't kill a fit forty-three year old. They need someone to carry the bodies. This is not the same thing as Tibby and mother.*" Sadly, Eddy did believe his uncle and brother would be killed, because of the sheer numbers coming into the camp. It was obvious that the slaves in this camp were marked for extermination. Old timers said that this was a, "*Vernichtungslager.*"

Eddy tried to hide his sadness. This was the last time Eddy saw his brother or uncle. Eddy volunteered himself by stepping forward. The SS officer looked at him like he was checking out livestock. "You are too young to be a tradesman," he said.

Eddy had heard from other prisoners that there was a current need for a glazier, someone to replace broken windows which riddled the walls of the factories. How information got exchanged, Eddy did not know, but the information had always turned out to be true.

"I worked over a year as a glazier, putting in windows," Eddy said in the most mature voice he could muster. It didn't matter if it was a lie. All he knew was that he wasn't going to stay where he was, and he knew also that he was a quick study and the other prisoners would help him with his ruse. The guard looked at Eddy again, "a glazier huh? What was your job?"

"I did it all. I cut glass, puttied when we had it and am good at framing," Eddy lied with confidence. The officer thought about it one more time and said finally, "Okay, go ahead."

So, Eddy joined the group that *stepped out*. He still didn't know what was happening next, but was hoping that he wouldn't be sent straight to the crematorium. He knew from experience that the Nazis never told the truth. Hadn't they already told everyone at the train station when culling the workers from the elderly, women and children, "*Don't worry. You'll see your families again later.*" They were lying to take lives. Eddy was lying to save his. He never saw his family again and never knew exactly what happened to them, leaving Eddy always to fill in the blanks of his knowledge with the worst possibilities.

Now, Eddy was practically giddy when those who had stepped out of line this time were told to gather their meager belongings and taken to the train station instead of straight to their deaths.

They put about seventy-five people into another wagon, no food or water. Eddy realized at that point that they were going to be a long time in this train.

Hershi was in that same train car. Eddy did not know what Spiegel had said to get selected, but they were both there.

"Did you bring anything to eat?" Eddy asked.

Hershi said that he had been given a small piece of bread and Eddy knew he would be able to share a portion.

He also knew that was all they would get to eat for a while, but at least this group was not marked for instant death, otherwise they would not have fed them at all.

This whole trip took about a day.

***

They had taken this seasoned batch of workers to a smaller camp. It was much smaller than Auschwitz. In the train, they didn't have guards on top as before, but there were three guards stationed inside the car now. There were however many guards all around by the time the doors of the train car were opened.

Immediately one of the guards at the second camp spoke Hungarian to the prisoners. "You know you guys just crawled out from the throat of death," he said matter-a-factly of Auschwitz, confirming for Eddy not only that he'd made the right decision, but that his brother and uncle had not.

No one in Eddy's group said a single word after the guard made his morbid proclamation…but Eddy already knew he was lucky. He thought of Karl and his uncle but tried not to show any emotion to the guards or other prisoners. Whenever anyone stood out, especially in a moment of weakness or humanity, that usually meant that you didn't see them again.

The prisoners got down from the train and as soon as a line was formed, they took everyone straight to take a shower.

As usual, the prisoners were being herded like animals but with that same irrational sense of urgency.

"Everyone undress! Now, Now, hurry, hurry, hurry," Eddy heard these commands in the distance as soon as they arrived at the new camp. Now the same phrases were being shouted directly at his group.

All the prisoners looked at each other, eyes wide, trying to conceal their thoughts that, *"Was this it...the **final** shower?"*

"It doesn't look like I'm going to make it out this time. Maybe the dream was wrong," Eddy thought, hoping that the words did not come out of his mouth. Luckily, this time it was just a shower. This was the first time in months that Ed had felt water running on skin. When he realized that it was not the end of his life, he looked around a little.

After removing all their clothes, shoes included the prisoners were commanded in the same bellowing shout that the German soldiers used for everything, "Leave your belongings outside!"

Methodically, but not too slowly Ed removed all his clothing and set everything in a pile outside the doorway of the large shower room.

The prisoners were taken in groups of 8 or 10 at a time into the shower room, which was directly adjacent to the open latrines. Next to Eddy in line was a heavy looking guy, kind of plump, but in an odd way. This guy seemed to be wearing a full apron that hung all the way around his torso, almost all the way to the ground.

Why was he wearing an apron? Why didn't the soldiers shoot him for disobeying?

It was then that Eddy realized that this apron was attached directly to this fellow's skin. *In fact, it was his skin!* Apparently, this guy had been a person of means when he was free, before he was taken into Auschwitz. Eddy reasoned that he had been one of those who could not support his great bulk on the food he'd been given. He had lost well over 100 pounds surviving on his meager meals, and the starvation diet had produced such rapid weight loss that the skin hadn't had time to shrink with the rest of the body. His skin hung down like an apron or dress to the delight of the soldiers who stood by, laughing and watching. The guy never twitched or displayed any reaction to the taunting. Eddy respected him for this and so, apparently did the rest of the prisoners, because none of them ever looked in his direction. They just pretended not to notice.

When Eddy came out from the shower he went to where he'd left his pile of belongings. The few items he had with him were still there except for the ones that he needed the most. His shoes were gone!

Eddy did not complain or ask what had happened or he chanced being punished, perhaps to death. So, he just got back into line and followed the instructions of the soldiers, barefoot.

Eddy had to hurry, the the men were getting assigned to a barracks and when his group was ready, they were hustled out. Eddy was amazed when he saw his new living arrangement. It was much less crowded than the first camp, with only two to four to a bunk!

The food was better too. At least there was food. In the mornings they were given black coffee for breakfast.

Hershi had *earned* the coveted job of making the coffee for all of the barracks. Two other inmates from each barracks would carry the large container of coffee to their barracks. Eddy had volunteered for the extra job of carrying the coffee. He was always up early and saw this as another potential opportunity.

Hershi had earned the job of making the coffee because his uncle had bribed the Kapo with a diamond to give his nephew a prime job.

When it was still dark outside, 5:30 or 5:45, they put the prisoners into an assembly line. The little guys were told to stand in the front, taller guys in the back. The guards then proceeded to check out the new workers. Twenty-five people were assigned to one type of work, Twenty-five to another type of work and so on until all the jobs had been matched with a prisoner.

***

Occasionally, Eddy had to stand barefoot in freezing weather because shoes were a valuable commodity and prisoners would come and go often. Even though it was March already, it was still bitterly cold, and snow stood in piles on the frosty ground. It reminded Eddy of the character building exercises his father and grandfather had put him through when they told him to strip naked in the snow and rub it on his body. "*I can stand it for the short walk to the factory,*" Eddy thought to himself, knowing that he'd endured worse in the past. "*But, I need to get some shoes soon.*"

***

He trusted his dream. Why not? He had nothing else of his own to hold onto. Also he knew that if an opportunity presented itself, it was in his nature to seize upon it. He always kept his eyes and ears open and decided to say very little. Although Eddy had claimed to be a glazier, he was sent to work in the refinery. It was hard work, but Eddy was used to that. The trouble was he had to unload bricks with his bare hands and hated it. He thought it would be tolerable if he had gloves to put on but never got a chance to fulfill that dream.

By the end of the first day of work, he had no skin on his hands. When he was done with work, his hands throbbed and ached. When he wasn't working the pain never ended. Every night his hands would be pulsing and throbbing. If it wasn't for the fact that prisoners were kept on the edge of total exhaustion at all times, the pain might have kept Eddy awake. Sometimes he would be assigned to a different job. Whatever the assignment, he just went where he was directed.

***

Sometimes Eddy would have to do the same job again the next day. If any prisoner refused to work, they were kicked and beaten in a big show in front of the rest of the prisoners and then hauled off to the crematorium if they didn't survive the beating.

So, if Eddy had to go back to the same bricklayer job for a second day, he just went where he was told and suffered in silence. Eddy didn't realize it at the time, but working the weaker prisoners to death was part of the plan. Complete extermination of *undesirables,* plain and simple was not always well excepted by the general public. However, it was easy to accept that if a prisoner or two or even *thousands* died in the line of duty to the larger *cause*...well, that was just the price of doing business. That is, of course as long as those lost were not German.

***

To Eddy it was also worth suffering for the benefit of regular albeit small amounts of food or a fairly comfortable place to sleep.

One bite of bread and an hour's sleep might be the difference between death and survival. There was a very slim margin for error.

At lunchtime (and there had not been a lunchtime previously in Auschwitz) they would be served potato peel soup. Ed was sure that the guards and kapos were getting the meat of the potato, but the skin was at least something substantial. The cooks would boil the potato peels in water with a little salt. Not much care was taken in the process.

Each of the workers were given a bowl and a spoon which they would carry to the pot. Every worker got a single scoop. If you were *liked* or had favor for whatever reason, then you got some skin. There was as much sand and grit in the soup as potato peel.

The Germans told the cooks not to bother cleaning the potato skins. These dirty skins were peeled from the potato and put directly into large pots of water, instead of being cleaned first. This dirty water concoction was the entire recipe for the soup. If they did *not* like you, then you got your scoop from the top of the pot, which had no real substance. Eddy felt that he was getting more dirt than peel at times, but didn't care. At least it was boiled.

"Move!" They would say after each portion was poured. "Hurry, Hurry up! Move, Move, Move!"

Eddy decided, *"Whatever the guy with the ladle gives me, he gives me."* Eddy didn't try to ask for any explanations or special attention. However, for some reason the guy doing the serving seemed to like Eddy. So Eddy was served his portion from the bottom of the pan. At night the skilled prisoners also got a little slice of German black bread, a little margarine, and another scoop of potato peel soup. It was as if the leaders of this camp didn't want their workers to die before being moved to a different place.

***

In this camp the skilled prisoners were also getting three cigarettes a week. Eddy did not smoke and instantly made the decision that he was going to keep it that way and trade the cigarettes as soon as he got them.

The Germans and the gypsies were given full packs. Eddy had observed that some guys were willing to trade food for cigarettes. "*Stupid guys,*" he thought. "They will not last."

Eddy therefore always got at least one extra daily ration of bread for his cigarettes. Those guys who bought the cigarettes from him were the ones who didn't last very long. They didn't survive even this camp.

One guy seemed to have a lot of strikes against him. He was a smoker, a big muscular Italian fellow and Eddy had heard it said that the guy was, "Wired like a Brillo Pad." The Brillo Pad was a new fangled invention that had been created in 1911 by an unlikely partnership between two New Yorkers, a Jewish attorney named Loeb, and a German aluminum manufacturer.

***

Eddy was at this camp about five and a half months. Sometimes, depending upon the season, instead of potato skins the prisoners were given some pea soup. For some reason, the pea soup was full of maggots floating on top. When the peas were heated, the maggots would float to the surface of the boiling water. Ed ate the maggots happily. When you are hungry to the point of starvation, you will eat anything remotely edible, including maggots because they provided a little extra protein.

Because there was so little food, some of the not-so-fortunate decided to eat grass or hay to keep their stomachs full. Eddy even even tried eating the bark off the trees on occasion. Generally, human digestion systems did not allow for much value being obtained from uncooked anything, let alone grass, hay, or bark.

Eddy's drive to survive went far beyond the family training of farming skills that he had learned from his father, grandfathers, and uncles. Eating bark, rats, insects, or other things not generally considered food had been a trait ignited in all the slaves. This primal desire to survive was born in that trial and error survival instinct that humans were known for and often turned deadly.

***

Another opportunity was created when he decided to get up early one morning and get the coffee for the barracks. This was another stroke of luck, as far as Eddy was concerned. While he was performing this volunteer task he knew he could steal the coffee grounds and once in a while, a real, whole potato. Once in a blue moon, the prisoners got powered milk and noodles along with a piece of salami made from horse meat. No matter what, handing out the food and drink put him in a respected position. The guards and Kapos saw this as a way to lessen their own responsibilities, while the prisoners, near starving all the time did not bite the hand that fed them. Eddy's hand was doing at least some of the feeding.

Another bonus at this new camp was that once a month the inmates were allowed another shower. The guards made sure that no one would linger by controlling the water temperature. Only seconds after a group entered the water always went from scalding hot to ice cold within a minute of a man starting to bathe. Months earlier lice had started to become epidemic.

***

From the moment Eddy had struck out on his own, he never complained. He kept away from other prisoners, but he would listen. They always told stories about food and dinners at home and Eddy didn't want to hear this kind of tale. He had made up his mind that one of the most important things he could do for his own sake was to try and not to dwell on his hunger. Or, even better was to actually not *be* hungry.

***

At this point, some of the other guys in the camp started dying off from various things or committing suicide. They couldn't take it. The bigger a guy was, the faster he died. "*A big, real strong guy needs more food than a skinny kid,*" Eddy reasoned, believing that this might help him slip through the cracks of that iron gate that he had seen in his dream. At least he knew that supplies were limited for everyone and *the skinny kid* was doing work and not eating food that now even the soldiers were wanting.

***

Each morning the barrack captains would tell the other inmates to drag out the bodies of those who did not make it through the night. The first time, it was a shock when Eddy saw a dead body, especially when he had talked to that same person when they were alive just the the night before. With each new death however, Eddy became more resolute that his dream was coming true. He thought to himself, "This won't happen to me."

In addition to the Jews who were marked for extermination, the camps always had a lot of German prisoners who were already tried and convicted of some other crime. A prisoner who had killed his wife and sister-in-law was in charge of Eddy's barracks. These prisoners were given the opportunity to join the Nazis, many in fact were released to join the fighting as soldiers.

In every camp there were also Russian prisoners. It was because of this guarded friendship that Eddy got a new pair of shoes only a couple of days after his had been stolen in the shower.

Eddy knew three Russian guys who had escaped through the factory. Escape was not at all tolerated and if it did happen, the escaped prisoner was made an example of in the most dramatic way that the local police, free citizens, and Third Reich soldiers could devise. The three Russians, everyone was told the next day, were caught right away.

The guards told everyone to *step out* into the yards near the barracks. Lines formed quickly as always. The townspeople were standing nearby and the Germans made a big deal out of thanking them for helping. The soldier said gleefully that the townspeople had captured, killed and brought three dead bodies back to the camp--claiming they were the Russians who had escaped. Except for the uniforms, there was no way of really telling that they were the Russians. Soldiers always wore the uniform of the enemy. These bodies were laying unceremoniously posed one across the other. The soldiers took a moment to reposition the bodies so that it could be seen that all three had lost their features. They had their faces shot off!

The camp commander was on hand, making the show complete. He gave congratulations and credit as he detailed how the local police and townspeople had effectively used Doom Doom bullets to pepper the escaping Russians. These types of bullets would shatter upon impact causing explosive and ragged wounds where ever they struck a victim. The wounds were not intended to allow healing.

The bodies were dragged to the nearby barracks wall and leaned against it. At this point, everyone was told to walk past them and take a good look at what happens to those who tried to escape.

Eddy walked silently past, but another friend Adolf Spiegel who Eddy had met in Auschwitz, turned away. He said he couldn't look at the bodies so he got beaten. When it appeared that the beating had made its point, Speigel was told to walk up to the bodies, as he was supposed to do to begin with.

But now, the commander knew he had to up the ante. He could have killed Speigel right there, but that would have only diminished the effect of the three dead Russians. He seemed to have a great idea. He told Spiegel he not only had to look, but he had to *take a real good look* and to kiss every one of the mutilated bodies on the place where their faces used to be.

With great struggle pausing at every one, the poor guy did as he was told. That guy remained friends with Ed when he came to the United States and opened Columbia Saving and Loan after the war.

***

Eddy was told to step out and help transport the bodies by pushing them in a cart to a nearby ditch, where they were doused with gasoline and lit ablaze.

"You," the SS soldier scanned a group and his eyes fell on Eddy.

These were the first dead bodies that Eddy was allowed to handle. He didn't know how many more would follow.

He determined that he was supposed to place the remnants of human beings, one by one onto the cart. While pushing the cart, Eddy saw and removed a pair of Russian knee high boots and pulled them over his frost bitten feet. There were no socks, and Eddy was plagued for months afterward with severe blisters. Though he felt it was possible that he would have lost his feet entirely if he hadn't gotten the boots, so he decided he was better off.

That night three other Russian prisoners had *found* a bottle of wood alcohol. There was no telling why, but all three died that night as well. Eddy heard that it was alcohol poisoning. Their skin had turned black.

***

They were there about five months in Duren Furt near Breslau. No prisoner could stay longer than six months in a place. Keeping the Jews off balance and wondering what would happen next was a part of the extermination plan, a tactic that started way back when Eddy and his family was placed in the Ghetto.

This second camp was south east of Breslau, and had about twenty five to thirty thousand prisoners. Then they suddenly moved everyone again down to the factory being bombed during the night. They took Eddy and all the men of his barracks northwest.

***

The third camp Funfteichen-Markstaedt had more than maybe fifty thousand prisoners and slaves. There were French, Russian and all kind of nationalities here. The camps always seemed to be on very flat land. This move took place in the middle of the summer. Eddy and the others had to march through open fields for about two or three miles in the morning on a beat up road that led to a factory. The factory was surrounded by a wire fence. That factory was operated by the Krupp and Speer manufacturing companies.

***

In all the camps, the slave laborers were called *Untermenchen* to indicate that they were less than human. This made it easier for the companies to pretend their *helping the war effort for the Third Reich was such a noble cause that it overshadowed the use of slave labor.*

Both companies that ran the factories were responsible for making ammunition, rockets, and other wartime products and weaponry. They were allowed to use the slave labor that the SS provided as a way of keeping the cost of production down. The Germans did not care if these companies worked their slaves to death. That was one less Jew that needed to be exterminated in the long run. Hitler's loyalists had convinced these and other manufacturers that helping the Fatherland and making a large profit were justification enough for any horrors inflicted on the *Untermenchen.*

Ukrainians and Russians also had been entangled in a long standing feud. So it was easy for the Germans to stir up old feelings of hatred and get the Ukrainians to cooperate against the *common enemy.*

***

There was an SS officer at this camp that openly hated Russians. From the beginning of Ed's incarceration, he saw Germans picking hapless Russians and punishing them for sport. They might pick an individual out of a workgroup and beat that guy until he was dead. One day this SS officer picked a Russian pilot, took him into a room and killed him with his bare hands. As always the prisoners were forced to watch.

That pilot, unknown to the SS officer however, had a lot of friends in the camp. Although this kind of incident was common place, for some reason these friends were not going to let this particular death go without a challenge. There were immediate stirrings in this case about *getting revenge*. Hope was stirred momentarily in Eddy's barrack, but it was short lived, even thought retribution in this case was swift.

The next day Eddy had to go relieve himself. The latrine was on one side of a barrack with a wash area on the other side. Three or four Russian guys were in the latrine when Eddy came in. They were just standing still and seemed to be waiting for something.

One said to Eddy when he entered, "Get back to the barracks."

It did not take a quick study like Eddy long to size up the situation. "No, I'm staying. I want to see," Eddy said. He wanted to see this SS officer get what was coming to him. To Eddy, like every other Jewish slave, it was personal.

"Okay," the Russian prisoner said. "But remember, I advised you to leave." The Russian prisoner who had spoken to Eddy, did not take his eyes off of the doorway to the latrine.

Ode to Life!

"Here he comes," he said abruptly and Eddy moved out of the way. As soon as the SS officer was close to the building they jumped him, pulling him into the latrine area. When they got to the toilet, they all grabbed him and then dropped the officer head first into the shit. He struggled weakly for a moment, but he was no match for the four strong Russians. The shit was so thick, the SS officer drowned pretty quickly. He went down like it was quicksand. Eddy and the four Russians left the latrine casually, not looking back or speaking to Eddy or one another.

Within ten minutes, the guards came running into the latrine and they pulled the SS officer's head out from the shit. Somehow they seemed to know where to look and what they were going to find. *Who had tipped them off?* Ed wondered.

There was no immediate retribution from the Germans, but everyone fully expected a serious reaction. Bodies were piling up daily without provocation. Everyone knew there would be a response, but all went to their work assignments as if nothing had happened.

That night, as expected the Germans decided that they needed to show who was in charge. They went through the barracks and told every Russian to *step out*.

They lined up every Russian, counted to ten, pulled out every tenth man, and immediately they were led to the nearby gallows and hanged or shot.

All the camps had crematoriums, and this one was no exception. They would burn the dead bodies every night.

People that were hanged, their eyeballs would pop out and the tongues would swell up. Eddy and the other prisoners would have to take the bodies to the crematorium. Eddy always seemed to be *volunteered* for the worst jobs and therefore he was constantly dealing with the disposal of dead bodies.

Ode to Life!

as told to Gordon Richiusa

Chapter Five
Fire & Ice

In 1943, while Eveline was in Belfair Orphanage, in Cleveland, it was decided that the *foreign children,* should be given the opportunity for success in the U.S. by learning English. To that end U.S. soldiers came to read Comic Books to the children on a regular basis.

Eveline only spoke French when she was rescued and brought to the U.S., so the comic book reading was probably a great way to teach her and the other children English.

In fact this was probably one of Eveline's most pleasant memories of soldiers during childhood. The orphanage was a mixed blessing for Eveline, though. She knew that all the other children had no parents.

However it was important to her that she was not. "I'm not an orphan. My parents are alive and will come to get me as soon as they can," she told anyone who would listen.

Naturally, most of the orphans told a similar story. It just so happened that Eveline and her two sisters had survived much to the credit of the eldest Jacqueline.

In 1943 Eveline moved into her first foster home along with her younger sister. Jackie had been placed into a foster home as soon as they arrived.

***

Ode to Life!

At about that same time, one day in October 1944, Eddy went to the factory as usual prepared for just about anything. He was not ready for the turn that his subservience would take on this day.

There was a daily diet of death in all the work-camps from Auschwitz to the moment of liberation almost two years later. There was a kind of irony to Eddy that each camp was so closely associated with a railway station, because one was the epitome of stability, while camp life was anything but stable.

Everyday more and more trains were loaded and unloaded. Death rode in and Death rode out. Bodies were moved toward the crematorium of those who died the night before. When the doors were opened to the cars filled with new slaves, first the dead bodies were pushed out and those on the docks disposed of them. Sometimes people simply gave up, perhaps forcing one of the SS to punish them to death. Sometimes a person would find another way to commit suicide.

There was no way to keep count of how many died each day. There was no way to get acquainted with a routine. As soon as you started to orient yourself to the number of prisoners, the time of year, the direction of the train tracks or anything else, it was time to move on. Everything was hurried. No requests were ever made. Commands came suddenly and in a rapid, staccato succession.

To desensitize the prisoners to this traumatic reality, camps were run with the legendary German precision and efficiency of a military exercise. Everything happened as if according to a well thought out Master Plan.

The days always started early, before the sunrise. That was acceptable to Eddy. He was used to rising before everyone else. Eddy would go and bring black coffee to his barracks.

A typical day was a series of life and death decisions. The Block Elders known as Kapos, would come to each barrack and shout, "Up. Up! Mach Snell. Get up. Get Dressed. Outside. Now, Now, Now." Short people in the front. Taller people in the back. This is where they would find out who was still alive. If you did not come out quickly, that was your choice. You might be killed.

"Everything in order?" The call went out to the Kapo, usually a big guy who was also a prisoner but received special treatment.

There was almost always at least one dead inside each barracks. When bodies were discovered, a few survivors were assigned to drag the bodies to the crematorium. Living and dead were counted. Numbers mattered to the Germans.

Sometimes the count of those who had gone into the barracks the night before did not jibe with what was found in the morning. Occasionally one or two had escaped and an immediate search party was sent out.

Ode to Life!

Whatever the day's assignment, there was always the air of death hanging over the survivors, both figuratively and literally. Outside the doorway of each barracks was always a gallows. Sometimes when someone had been murdered by their captors the body was left to hang for a day or two so that all could see it. There were days when more than one barracks had a body hanging outside. It was important to the Germans to make a show of all torture and death. They wanted the survivors to be saturated in the possibility of dying at any capricious moment.

The SS officer in charge randomly assigned jobs, though prisoners were always in the same place in line, in the parade yard just outside the barracks. "You five," he would point. Pick up bodies. You five, go to the factory. You three dig ditches. You, you, you…" assignments came fast but in monotone.

Sometimes during raids, the slaves were forced to leave the barracks and stand in ditches for hours. The ditches would have gathered freezing water in the bottom, sometimes deep enough to cover up to their knees. Since Eddy was small, he would crawl under the bunk and go back to sleep. No one checked during raids. He knew if he had been caught, he would be killed but he didn't care. His reasoning was that if he had to stand in freezing water, he might have died as a result of the frostbite anyway. After the raids, he would crawl back into the bunk, knowing that if he did not, again, he would be killed in the morning.

When the commanding officer would line up the prisoners in the courtyard and begin assigning work details was the time that revealed just how many thousands of poor souls had been immorally arrested. Each barrack stood in the cleared area outside, in rows similar to the way they were stacked in their bunks.

Depending upon the size of the camp there were hundreds to almost a thousand packed into a single barracks. Now, like a defeated army thousands stood. Some of those who were unwilling to experience anymore horror would suddenly break ranks, and run at full speed toward the fences which had been erected to prevent escape. They were essentially committing suicide, the act that Eddy's mother tried on board the train before arriving at Auschwitz.

The perimeters were set up in layers and staggered, and even altered from camp to camp so that the order of fencing, or barbed wire, or guard towers, or patrols with dogs could not be shared from camp to camp.

Daily there were bodies hanging from the barbed wire or from the gallows when the prisoners went outside. No one knew the actual method that Death had chosen for these poor souls or where or when they had died. The bodies could have come from anywhere. However, the bodies hung like banners to ensure that the slaves stayed desensitized to the horrors of mindless, cruel death.

Work details were always changing.

Ode to Life!

On this day, the officer walked lazily in front of the ranks, pointed to Ed and said, "You will do."

Immediately he was seized, two officers and two kapos. They took him to an experimental area, nonchalantly gave him a shower in a nearby field shower. The shower all by itself made him suspicious, but he knew that speaking out would probably get him immediate and very negative attention.

Eddy suddenly realized that this was not something he wanted to volunteer for. Suddenly they lifted his skinny body with eight hands, placed him on a makeshift wooden table where they held him, then tied down his legs, head and hands. It looked like they were preparing to operate, which was confirmed when a Jewish doctor prisoner and about a dozen SS officers were brought into the hut.

The commanding officer, in a psychotically calm voice was telling the others in German that this practice-procedure was going to help German soldiers if they needed to perform a similar operation in the field. They wanted to see how someone would react to surgery without an operating room, proper supplies (such as blood for transfusions) or anesthetic. They also wanted to evaluate the ability of the human body—such as one was living under strained conditions like those found on a battlefield—to heal without antibiotics or bandages. They just didn't have enough confidence to test their technique on Germans, so they used the slaves who they had convinced themselves were *less than*.

Time lagged, allowing Eddy to feel every cut and the pressure of his bindings. When the cutting was done, they brought bags of ice and put them where Eddy's perfectly healthy appendix used to be.

Eddy struggled at first but his limbs, torso, and head were all strapped to the table. The surgeon picked up a tiny scalpel and seemed to show it to Eddy. He smiled and Eddy closed his eyes. He didn't feel the first deep cut because of the ice at the surface of his skin, but as the knife dug deeper, there came a searing pain through Eddy's abdomen, as if he were being set on fire. The sound was exactly the same as Eddy remembered when a pig was being slaughtered.

Eddy screamed again and again, and fought, and pulled against his bindings, but no one paid any attention and the orderlies only held him down more tightly to the table.

In a matter of a few minutes, they took out Eddy's appendix. During the whole procedure and afterward, he never lost consciousness. He did not faint, so was awake the whole time. It was the most excruciating pain he'd ever felt and wished for unconsciousness, but it never came.

When the surgery was finished they sewed Eddy up and instead of more ice, they put little bags of wet sand on the wound to hold it closed and slow the bleeding.

Only minutes later Eddy was carried into a bigger, attached room and put onto a proper cot. One of the doctors, who was also a Jewish prisoner had been ordered to assist in the operation. He stayed by Eddy's side and monitored his recovery. When Eddy was tied to his new cot and the two were alone he whispered to Eddy in a congratulatory tone, "Boy, you are very strong."

Eddy did not respond and was there, under observation for about four days. Every part of his body was traumatized. He couldn't even swallow his own saliva because everything was burning inside. Occasionally ice packs were placed on the slowly healing wound, but nothing was given for the pain.

As the Nazis wanted to see if anyone, especially a soldier in the field, could survive this type of operation they were hedging their bets by using the little, Jewish teenager.

Eddy wasn't going to give in. Everything burned inside him, but he kept fighting. He tried to keep his mind occupied on other things. He dreamed about being back home in his village, with his friends, doing his chores. He remembered his dream and went over it in his head again and again, searching for details, anything to take his attention away from the searing pain.

After a few days the pain subsided a bit, and Eddy was told to get dressed and report to his work assignment. He walked sideways for months while his wound, untreated, was still healing. It hurt to stand straight and he didn't want to pull out his crude stitches. It felt like his insides were on fire for about two more weeks after this torture, but Eddy never gave up and he certainly wasn't going to give in now.

***

There were guards stationed both inside and outside the fences at all times. One freezing day, a German soldier in one guard post told Eddy to pick up some wood for the fire and bring it to him. "Hey, I'm freezing my ass off here!"

In order to do what he was being asked, Eddy had to open the gate that separated *outside the camp* from *inside*.

The guard from another tower saw Eddy and yelled, "You are out of bounds!" Eddy was too far away to clearly understand the meaning of the guards words, but he knew what he was saying.

Eddy hurriedly had already picked up wood inside the fence and was carrying it to the fire on the outside of the guard post. The shouting was less a warning than an explanation of what happened next.

Before Eddy or the soldier who had ordered Eddy to pick up the wood could respond, the second guard aimed his rifle and shot at Eddy. Eddy felt the bullet pass by his face. The guard now was yelling, "He's trying to escape!"

The shout brought a third SS officer running.

"You tried to run away huh?"

"No, sir, I was asked to get some wood."

The SS officer looked at the 2nd guard. "Did you ask this guy to go outside the fence?"

"No I didn't ask him," the guard lied.

The guard wasn't supposed to tell Eddy to get the wood anyway.

The SS officer wrote down Eddy's number. When that happened, Eddy figured that it was all over. He knew from

Ode to Life!

experience and stories from the others that when they took your number down you should just give up. Anonymity was safety. When your number was record that meant you were just as good as dead.

When Eddy got back to camp, he said to his friend Spiegel, "You know, probably they will call my number out. Don't worry, I will see you later." He was thinking positive because of the dream.

When *later* came, they did call Eddy's number. He stepped forward and saw the ropes hanging. They lined up all those who had be selected as examples under ropes in front of all the prisoners. Everyone was forced to watch so that they would be reminded of how close death was at all times.

There were eighteen men of all sizes being called out. Eddy was the seventeenth in line. He had moved into position and felt without looking up a noose hanging above his head. He stood there waiting.

An SS officer came to inspect everyone before execution and walked by Eddy. He said, "How old are you?"

Bumi said, "Fifteen."

The officer looked at him only briefly, as seeing each slave as a person probably caused what happened next, "Too young to be hanged today," he said.

Then, in the same breath the SS officer pronounced a new sentence while tipping his head toward Eddy, "Twenty five lashings."

Eddy never knew why he was spared the noose, but could not help but speculate about the motivations of the officer's decision to let him live. Maybe the officer thought the camp could get more work out of the teenager; maybe he had a child Eddy's age. Eddy did not know.

He was taken outside and his shirt removed while they placed him into a wooden yoke. Two Kapos came forward with short rubber hoses. The hoses had wire threaded through the middle, to prevent the hose from breaking prematurely. It would not do much for the fear factor, if beatings ended with the makeshift whip falling apart.

The fear factor was in a sense more important than the punishments themselves, especially for the onlookers as those who were hung or beaten to death would not be much of a deterrent after they bodies were removed. So, they made a show of Eddy's beating. They clamped him into a yolk, near the same gallows that he just previously was going to be hung from. They counted every lash out loud.

"Eins, Zwei, Drei, Vier!"

Ed did his best to ignore the lashings, but he felt the first four, one from each of the men who had been called forward to administer the beating. "*One, Two, Three, Four*"

Eddy never lost consciousness, almost satisfied, knowing at least that he wasn't going to be hanged that day.

A couple of prisoners helped him back to the barracks. Two doctors who were prisoners put cold rags on his back all night long.

Ode to Life!

as told to Gordon Richiusa

Chapter Six
Merry Christmas

It was Christmas time and Eddy was still hanging onto survival in his third camp. The head of the German SS at the camp, for some unknown reason had decided to give all prisoners a proper meal because it was Christmas. While the officers and other favored prisoners were eating much more substantial food most of the time, the war had obviously compromised supply lines. So when the camp commandant decided to give everyone some bread and a big scoop of beef stew, Ed was suspicious but asked no questions.

Instead, he thought to himself, *"I'll eat the bread and I'll save the beef stew for later."* He knew that he needed to portion it out over a couple of days. He was constantly hungry.

Before the meal a group of prisoners had volunteered to entertain, about a dozen. Some men dressed up as women, quite a few as Frenchmen, vaudeville like. The commandant walked by and wished everyone a Merry Christmas, even though almost everyone in the barracks was there because they were Jewish. With a nod of his head, they commenced the entertainment,

The prisoners were lined up and served as if this were any other meal. Most ate the beef stew as if they were starving, because they were, in all cases, at least on the verge of starvation.

Eddy naturally cautious took his big scoop of beef stew and went off to the side and covered it. The bread was more of a ration than he was used to, but he ate slowly. Not many spoke or made a sound while they ate. Before everyone had finished being served, the first prisoner who had eaten his whole portion ran outside. Eddy noticed that this poor guys stomach had blown up like a balloon, like cows eating uncooked clover, and he could hear retching and moaning sounds coming from just outside the door of the barrack. Then a stampede began.

Everyone that Eddy noticed was having explosive vomiting and diarrhea. Some got so sick that they died on the spot. They hadn't had real food for so long, their stomachs could not take it. By the end of the meal, there was human feces and vomit everywhere. Everyone had lost it.

The next morning the floors were covered. Eddy and some others who were not too sick to stand, were ordered to clean up the mess. Solving the problem as best they could, they filled buckets of water, one at a time from a pump outside and brought them into the barracks. Starting at the back of the barracks and working toward the doorway the whole area was washed down in the most crude manner. There was really no other way to remove the sea of diarrhea and vomit that now covered the floor and filled the barracks.

as told to Gordon Richiusa

***

Eddy had gotten friendly with some people from his hometown who were now prisoners in the same camp he was. They had been moving from camp to camp together. Only one of them had died from malnutrition. When this had happened, Eddy became unusually upset because the guy was from his home. Now, in light of what he'd seen and experienced the irony escaped him, but he was too weak to be angry, and besides, he still had his beef stew which he decided not to eat for fear of getting sick as the others did.

Shortly after this, Eddy was working outside the factory, shoveling coal, and doing other menial jobs. Every day was something different. This, Eddy realized was part of the effectiveness of the plan. The Germans did not want the prisoners to have any idea what was happening. They didn't want the slaves to be in one place for any length of time. They didn't want the *less than humans* to make friends, or stumble across someone who may have information about their families or the outside world.

However, within this atmosphere the other prisoners seemed to work around Eddy. One man met Eddy when he took his turn near the stone exhaust channel inside the barracks that gave off a little heat. Eddy did not know where the heat was coming from and decided it was probably better not to think about it, but everyone was happy to get a little warmth on a daily basis. This guy sat next to Eddy and immediately gave his name.

"Eugene Spiegel" Eddy's nickname for him was "Hershi".

"Adolf Hoffman," Eddy said with mock formality.

"You don't have any family with you?"

"No," Eddy said sadly, trying not to show how much that question hurt. Eddy decided that his turn at the hearth was over and he went back to his bunk. Months after Eddy got liberated, he stumbled across a new friend, Ignac Deutsch in Prague. They were shipped on the same plane from Prague to Northern Ireland together. They were also together in England.

Eddy and he remained friends and when they met again in America, Eddy was invited to be Ignac's best man at his wedding in Montreal. Ignac had many cousins who had changed their name from Deutsch to Namath. One of them became a famous football player by the name of Joe Namath.

***

The technique of normalizing chaos had been of real value to the Germans when they began the sorting of people. But now, more than 8 months a slave, it was clear that some outside forces were affecting the behavior of the German soldiers. The sounds of very heavy bombing came and went and came again. Word from workers who arrived daily on the trains which were always coming and going, was that one particularly loud explosion was from big munitions factory of Krupp and Speers being bombed. The day after the explosion, Eddy and the rest were put again onto cattle cars and taken to what would be for Eddy, The Fourth Prison Camp.

***

This fourth camp was at Durno, closer to Auschwitz in a part of Poland. The Russians could be heard coming closer. At this camp the slaves worked in the coal mines.

Eddy was here only four weeks, but long enough for typhus to break out, a disease often associated with insect transmissions, such as lice. There always seemed to be a high incidence of this disease during famine and war.

At this camp imprisoned doctors were given vaccines from the Germans to inoculate the healthy prisoners so they could go into the coal mines and continue working 24/7. Clothing of the prisoners was infested with lice all through the camp.

Eddy made the connection quickly when the doctor came into the barracks and gave him a vaccine. Since Eddy was highly infested with clothes lice, he immediately went outside and found a gas can that someone had left laying around near an engine for pulling coal. He poured the gas into a bucket that was used for mopping up, took off his cotton uniform and dunked it into the gasoline. He didn't have lice for a long time after that and never came down with typhus. All the seams of everyone's ragged clothing were full of white lice eggs and lice.

All of a sudden artillery fire was heard from a distance. Russians were getting closer. The Germans decided to move the whole camp. This is the time that has come to be known as *The Death March.* The slaves were given no food but sometimes one red beet a day each. The snow supplied the water needed. It was freezing cold. Every day many would die. They marched from two in the morning straight through the day until midnight. If a slave fell down they were killed. Eddy and the others were marched in rows of five across.

***

The German women from the village had been assigned the task of building concrete barricades to keep the advancing Russian army at bay as the numbers of soldiers and able bodied men seemed to be less and less. When the women worked they were laughing and singing songs, oblivious to the fact that the SS were leaving them behind. All the German civilians were being left behind.

While walking through one of the towns, Eddy found a pile of concrete, paper bags that had been discarded but not disposed of completely. He picked one up without stopping his march and with his bare hands tore a hold for his head and arms and slipped this under his uniform of rags. Some others saw what was happening and followed Eddy's idea. Eddy felt warmer now, but the concrete mix had left particles of lye that irritated his skin. Everyone kept his bag on anyway, since it was still very cold, and dying from freezing was much more likely than dying from skin irritation at this point.

They kept moving.

Relentlessly they drove the slaves. There was no feeling of *forward* or *backward*. Everyone was just moving to the command of the SS officers in charge of the march.

Eddy, and other slaves took turns sleeping while they marched. Eddy locked arms with the men on either side of him and immediately fell asleep. This was around 2:00 a.m.

Eddy slept the entire time hooked unto these two men. He awoke around 7:00 a.m. Eddy was not sure who was who anymore. There was a kind of sense of belonging now to the people who were around you. The longer they marched, the more Eddy felt this. He couldn't see the end of the line. There were thousands being marched toward the Czech border. The line was miles long.

A small group veered out of line toward the side of the road suddenly. At first Eddy just watched, but then he realized that these prisoners had broken ranks for a reason. There was a recently dead horse laying in the gutter that lined the dirt road. When Eddy realized what was happening he joined the twenty or so prisoners who were making the decision to eat anything they could find to stave off starvation-death.

Indiscriminate shots were fired by the SS guards shouting "back in line, back in line" killing and wounding some. Those who had broken ranks were driven back to their places in line. Eddy and others had grabbed and torn pieces of horse flesh from the carcass before returning to the line. Eddy offered some to the French doctor who commented casually before he devoured this gift, "You're bleeding."

Eddy had been shot. A bullet had grazed him along the back and blood was dripping from under the concrete bag. The doctor took a roll of crepe paper from some hidden place and began to wrap it around the wound. Eddy never knew where the doctor had obtained this party streamer. It came in handy now though, even as the bullet had only grazed Eddy, and this was not the worst wound he'd experienced during his enslavement, he was glad that the doctor was tending to him.

The thousands of slaves began to be prodded relentlessly, cruelly, inhumanly forward once again.

***

At one point, when cannon fire seemed to be very close, they came to a farm with a gigantic barn. Hundreds of slaves were crowded into the barn, which also had a loft. Some climbed up to the loft. Eddy didn't know where everyone was. He only knew that the barn was full, but not completely. There was enough room for some to sit or lay down in shifts.

The doors of the barn were locked and when they opened four or five days later, the biggest guys were told to dig a large hole on the side of the barn. Twenty or thirty people had died in the barn. Eddy was again selected to take the dead bodies from the barn and place them into the newly dug hole, which he did.

While moving bodies, Eddy noticed that some of those who had been pronounced "dead" were moving their eyes. At first Eddy thought it was an illusion spawned by exhaustion, but two of them looked directly into Eddy's gaze in a pleading way. Eddy said to the SS officer in charge, "These guys are not dead."

"Put them in the hole," the SS guard shouted at Eddy. "If you don't, then you'll have to join them."

The two that Eddy had thought alive had closed their eyes and were laying still, probably realizing that their fate was sealed and not wanting to drag anyone else down into the hole with them.

The prisoners were not allowed to speak, but everyone had learned to speak with their eyes and with gestures. When Eddy came from behind the barn on the final trip, he took his place in front of the line where the rest of the survivors had been gathered.

The farmer who had been in the nearby house Eddy assumed, came up and gave Eddy a wrapping of paper. A woman in the window of the nearby farmhouse, Eddy also assumed it was the farmer's wife, was there gesturing for Eddy to "Eat, Eat!"

When he looked inside the paper, he found quite a few freshly made dumplings. Immediately, Eddy took one of the dumplings and bit into it. He was starving but didn't realize it, and this one bite had an immediate reaction...like a bolt of lightning running through his body. He could feel responses from every part of his being. He also gave some to the doctor, Spiegel, and a few other friends. who were standing nearby. Eddy was happy to share. The French Doctor, from that point onward always stayed next to Eddy. It was the 21st of February, Eddy's birthday.

***

From the farm, Eddy and the rest of the slaves were marched to the railroad station and onto cattle cars, seventy-five in each open air wagon. Now the train began to move and everyday, one, two, three more were dead. As more died, Eddy and others put corpse on top of each other so they would be able to sit and sleep on the corpses. They rode in these death cattle cars for four or five days, or longer, everyone had lost track of time as far as Ed could tell. Again, there was no food given to the prisoners by the guards except for a little spam and a piece of bread the first day.

However, whenever the open train moved under bridges or through towns with two story buildings near the tracks, Eddy noticed that something curious was happening. If the town was a Czech town, people threw food into the cars as they past by. When the cars passed a German town, nothing was thrown into the trains. Czech then German village, one after another. Germans gave nothing. Czechoslovakians did. The rain and snow provided water. Ed had an aluminum bowl and caught water when he could. Every prisoner had a blanket rolled up and put across his back. Stop and Go...Stop and Go...Another military train passed in the opposite direction, all Hungarians. Hungary had been completely taken over by Germany by then.

The French doctor--Eddy never knew his name he just called him *Frenchy*—was standing next to Eddy, who was sitting on two bodies. These bodies were now not considered human, but the remains of poor souls who could simply not take anymore torture.

Eddy had covered these bodies with a blanket, still trying to offer some respect, but there was simply no room and sitting was always better than standing, since no one knew what was coming next, perhaps weeks of marching.

Eddy looked up at the Frenchman and offered to change places with him, giving the Frenchman a chance to sit for a while.

Thirty seconds later, a round of machine gun fire was launched from a Russian plane that passed over head. The SS who were guarding the prisoners crawled under the car and used the prisoners for cover. Eddy leaned down and commented to the Frenchman. "I hope these guys see that we are just prisoners."

There was no response. Eddy looked down at the Frenchman and tapped his shoulder. "Hey, didn't you hear me?"

Eddy did not know if the Frenchman had heard the question. His eyes were still open. He was looking straight ahead, but he was dead, sitting in the place that Eddy had been only one minute before. A bullet came through the wood and hit Frenchy in the back.

Ode to Life!

***

At the end of February the train stopped abruptly. They had arrived at Eddy's fifth camp, Dachau. The prisoners had no idea that this was literally the end of the line for them all. Clues were many that Germany was not doing well aside from the constant bombing and air attacks, as well as the lack of shouting from the guards.

"Off, off. Now, now, now," the shouting commands started suddenly. The prisoners were so weak, it took all their strength just to get out of the wagons. This led to the prisoners realizing that while they had come to another camp, they specifically had no place else to go. There was no room in any of the barracks. Ed and those who arrived were forced to stay in an open parade ground for the next three days. There was no free barracks or bunk space.

***

After three days, the prisoners were loaded back into the same uncleaned wagons that they arrived. They were on their way to Ebensee

At each new camp, as new prisoners came in, they were forced to sleep outside in the freezing cold.

No one knew anything for sure, but somehow rumors started that the Germans were getting rid of evidence. They didn't know that Hitler had ordered everyone killed, indiscriminately, regardless of whose side they were on. He was angry that the people in the German towns hadn't done enough to save the Fatherland. Naturally, there was little incentive to carry out these orders, but the Germans started carving out tunnels nearby to *hide rockets*, they said.

***

There were about 25,000 prisoners now with Eddy. Everyone had learned not to trust anything that the Nazis said.

For whatever reason, those in charge decided to move Eddy's group once again. Sorting was easier since Eddy's group was still in the open and easy to count and move. Deaths continued to occur daily and Eddy was always chosen to move the bodies, mostly into ditches or hastily dug mass graves. There was no way to simply kill everyone.

***

Another train ride and they ended up at Ebensee, a smaller camp in Austria. The Germans still believed that they needed slave workers for manufacturing the V1 and V2 rockets. Eddy was ordered back to work, where he went every day into tunnels and worked on digging out the dynamited rocks.

The workers used dynamite with very little safeguards, placing sticks into small holes that were dug into the rocks, lighting fuses and running out, the objective was to explode the rocks, then take the debris in carts. There were no tools except for the carts where they placed the rocks to dump them outside on the side of a nearby road.

The holes grew quickly into shallow caves, then tunnels until they were large enough to drive several trucks into.

Ode to Life!

Between moving carts of rocks and carts of bodies, Eddy was exhausted as usual, but did not get any relief from the madness when he returned to his barracks at night.

This barrack was ruled by a German prisoner, who in real life had been a professional killer.

Perhaps because he was trying to prove his worthiness, this officer was very enthusiastic about his job and took special pleasure in killing. There were two or three Kapos with him at all times, who did his psychotic bidding without question.

There was a large barrel of water outside the only barracks door, next to a special private gallows that this officer had decided he needed to have for his own personal use. He proudly called it his *hanging tree,* though it was not a tree at all. It was just a spot, near the door where an occasional, hapless soul would be sacrificed as an example to both those inside and outside the barracks. Even at this late date, the insane cruelty went unchecked.

And, of course daily supplies were being more and more compromised by the advancing Russian and American armies. Now, even the SS themselves were having trouble getting basic foods.

When the Italian government decided that their allegiance to the Third Reich was no longer possible, they gave up. General Dwight Eisenhower publicly announced Italy's surrender near the beginning of September, 1943. Germany immediately reacted with what they called, Operation Axis.

Mussolini had been deposed from power in an earlier collapse of the fascist government in July. The man who had filled the void of office was Pietro Badoglio, at the request of King Victor Emanuel; Badoglio negotiated a surrender that allowed the Allied troops to launch Operation Avalanche, a full on invasion of Italy, landing in Salerno.

The Germans were able to also snap into action, as Hitler had been making plans to invade Italy since Mussolini had begun to falter. General Badoglio fled from Rome with the Royal Family to southeastern Italy to begin the work of setting up an anti-facist Italian Government. Germany launched Operation Axis.

An Italian battleship, *Roma* became the first ship ever sunk by the new technology of a radio controlled guided missile, where more than 1,500 crewmen were drowned. When their former allies the Germans tried to move the Italian military into POW work camps, some escaped and volunteered to fight along side the Italian resistance in the North. Others had resisted—as was the case with Greece earlier—but they had been slaughtered by the Germans. When the Italian soldiers began surrendering to their former German allies, they were murdered by the thousands. The *lucky ones* were imprisoned in the same camps as the Jews and others who Hitler considered inferior. These former Italian soldiers remained in their military uniforms, since prison uniforms were not available any longer.

Ode to Life!

One day when Eddy was told to move bodies for disposal, he saw something more disturbing to him than any of the atrocities he'd been forced to witness thus far.

Several partially clad, or completely naked bodies that Eddy believed were obviously Italian soldiers, were laying face down in rows, mutilated in a weird, systematic manner. Their buttocks and been removed.

Eddy. working with another prisoner paused at the sight and was informed, "The Germans are starving too."

Eddy realized what this meant. Cannibalism had broken out in the camp. There were rumors of the Russian prisoners being the instigators of this, but without any other meat available, the SS officers probably also decided to taste the flesh of their former allies.

***

On the 4th or 5th of May, just before the SS disappeared, in the morning, the slaves were called out to the assembly yard but not sent to work. The commandant of Ebensee came out, "Everyone, I want you to go into the tunnels!"

He told everyone that this was happening *to keep everyone safe from the bombing and the fighting* that was expected to take place inside the fences.

These were the same tunnels that the slaves were forced to dig during their internment. The Germans could build and hide the V-1 and V-2 rockets there.

"Everyone, you will be safer inside!"

The reasoning that there was going to be bullets flying and fighting in the camp was not taken as the commandant had hoped. Everyone started hollering in a newly discovered solidarity, "No, we won't go!"

Somehow the word was passed amongst the prisoners to say *no* if they were asked to go to the caves. They had the feeling that either the Americans or the Russians were close to the camp. The commandant slinked away and disappeared.

That afternoon around 4:00, all the entrances at the tunnels exploded. The SS had set charges in the mouths of the tunnels. There were seven tunnels so that the Germans could hide what they were doing. For a long time, the Germans were planning on building the rockets--what they felt was a strategic military advantage *inside* the mountain.

The commandant, like all the rest in the dying Third Reich hierarchy, knew they could not kill everyone. They knew they were losing and that there would likely be retribution.

So he, and the entire SS support troops took the cowards way out and simply began to disappear. The guards at the gates were no longer standing their posts, and the next morning it was local police guarding the gates. The SS was mostly gone.

Unbeknownst to the slaves, local police had been ordered to take over all the camps and factories, and *kill everybody,* including even those Germans who had not performed to the high level that was expected by the Reich.

The Germans did not want to leave any trace of what they'd done, but there still was a sense of superiority and destiny.

The Jews had been condemned for the usual reasons. The German people and other allies to the Reich were being condemned because they didn't put up enough of a fight on behalf of Hitler's insanity. The camps were now running on autopilot. No one wanted to take any responsibility. At night, the last of the SS slipped into the darkness.

***

On the 6th of May, American troops came through the camps in trucks. Stopping at the center of the camp in a show of strength. The prisoners could not believe their eyes and ears.

"Liberation! You're FREE!"

"Felszabadulás! Szabad vagy."

"Freedom!"

"Svoboda!"

"Liberta!"

"свобода!"

"Freiheit!"

"Liberte"

"אנחנו סוף סוף חופשיים"

"FREEDOM! FREE! FREE! FREE!"

The sounds and the words of shouting now had a different, healing tenor, even within the confusion of languages. There was a moment when it seemed like things were calming down. The marching slowed. Uncertainty creeped back into the shouting.

Then, all at once, the realization that all the former enslaved prisoners were now free citizens once again spawned a sudden wild jubilation, somewhere between joy and disbelief. National anthems were sung, one over the other.

The slaves were being liberated in every language but with a common understanding.

***

When Eddy and some friends from his barrack wandered out into the open area between the barracks, the first thing Eddy noticed was that everyone started gathering in groups under and around flags of each country that had suddenly appeared.

Eddy saw the flag of Czechoslovakia and also flags about a dozen different countries. *Where had all the flags come from?* Eddy wondered. Were they hidden by the prisoners? Did the Americans bring different country flags with them? It almost seemed like an Olympics Closing Ceremony but then Eddy noticed that these banners were nothing but homemade flags, rags and strips of cloth which had been squirreled away by the various prisoners.

There was wild cheering, everyone happy beyond belief. Some marched aimlessly, others as if on parade around and around the camp with their flags, everyone singing their national anthems. All of the SS had disappeared earlier, as the Allied Command had advanced.

Ode to Life!

The Germans left the job of running the camps to the local people, who had not wanted to accept the job but now it was clear to everyone that Germany had been defeated.

The German people were dumbfounded. Even when they could hear loud cannon fire approaching, and see tanks in the distance while the streets were being readied to repel the advancing conquerers, the German people simply did not let the concept of defeat enter their minds. They could not conceive that they had lost the war that they were responsible for starting. They also miscalculated their ability to dominate the Russians. This miscalculation led to a misguided attack on the Russian Army, in their Russian homeland, in the middle of winter.

This is not an area of the world where the word freezing has the usual meaning. The Russians had wisely hidden their tanks and heavy equipment underground to be used later. The Russians knew that it was so cold that even trying to start a motor vehicle was foolhardy.

When Hitler decided that he wanted to finally settle old scores and attack Russia he did it in the middle of winter. Nothing worked. The Russians didn't have to use explosives in some cases, opting instead to bomb equipment from the air with water. Instantly, with the thermometer going down to minus 100, water was all that was needed. Soldiers and equipment were literally frozen in their tracks.

***

The Russian prisoners were all formerly members of the Russian Army. When any Russian caught or captured a German, castrations and mutilations were common. During the night, some of the last SS officers in the camp had obtained civilian clothes and escaped into the countryside. Only one day into the liberation, one of Eddy's friends from the barracks was looking around to see what was happening. It was late morning.

"Let's see if we can walk out of the gate," Eddy said to his friend. The two of them strolled out the gate and made a left turn. Eddy saw three young men dressed in civilian clothes walking toward the gates, back to camp with a formal but furtive stride. There was about a half dozen other Russian prisoners also outside and they took a special interest in these guys. They blocked the way of the guys heading back and one of the bigger Russians took their hands and examined them.

"Let us look at your hands," The former Russian prisoners demanded. Eddy was close enough that he noticed that there was an imprint on the left hand of one of the young men indicating that for some reason he had removed a recently worn ring to blend in.

The Russians grabbed hold and looked at the other's hands. There were marks on all their ring fingers, as if they had recently removed a band to hide their identity.

Eddy did not know who these guys were, reasoning that they may be former prisoners or townspeople who were just trying to protect their jewelry. The Russians seemed to know better and responded quickly, "These guys are SS officers" They had removed their swastika rings, hidden their rings in the barracks and were probably coming back to try to retrieve this and other items that they'd stashed.

Eddy had found, earlier, some of these same rings in the barracks the morning that they were originally liberated. The SS officers wanted to get away and not be noticed. Why they were trying to sneak back into the camp, was anybody's guess. Perhaps they had hidden some of Adolf Speigel's bribery diamonds somewhere and in their haste to escape had been unable to retrieve them. Eddy never knew for sure but he didn't have time to speculate now.

Everything happened very fast. The Russians now swiftly revealed knives, holding them to the faces of the SS spies, while the others held these three. The two with the knives quickly and without passion slit their throats.

There was blood everywhere and the sound was horrible. There was a mixture of gurgling and the unmistakable sound of flesh being cut. It reminded Eddy of what it sounded like when a pig was slaughtered.

The three men did not die instantly but wobbled around for a moment, until they lost so much blood that they fell dead. One had fallen into a ditch that had previously been used for disposal of the dead coming into the camp. The other two were helped along as well with prodding kicks.

Suddenly it was as if a switch had been thrown. When the ex-prisoners saw what the Russians had done, it spawned a series of executions, a blood lust of retribution for every horror and indignity that the SS had set upon the slaves. Kapos and others were rounded up and formally executed in a kangaroo style court.

The former German prisoner who had become the officer in charge of Eddy's barracks was one of those captured and dragged, kicking and screaming to his torturous death at a fire spit. Screams and the smell of blood filled the air. It was like a scene from Hell.

In the midst of the pandemonium which lasted well into the night, Eddy moved into position next to the body that had been kicked into the trench on the side of the road. He had become immune to handling dead bodies and noticed that this corpse of the German SS who had just had his throat cut was wearing a pair of finely crafted, knee high boots. They appeared to be Eddy's size, so he removed them and put them on his feet.

The rioting and carnage lasted on into the night. The American soldiers never tried to interfere. While the torture and executions continued into the wee hours, Eddy went back to the barracks, onto his bunk and went to sleep. Most of the others eventually joined him.

There was, as yet, no where else to go.

Ode to Life!

as told to Gordon Richiusa

Chapter Seven
New Life

After they were liberated, the prisoners were slowly nursed to health while the conquering armies debated on what would happen next. The liberated were fed milk and noodles at first, because the American liberators realized that a sudden change of diet for those who had eaten almost nothing for years could be fatal.

There was not enough fresh clothing at first to go around, so all the liberated were sprayed for lice and forced to wear the same clothes that they had, some for years. In a much more humane and orderly fashion tens of thousands passed through the spray area, that had once been one of the stations of shame for those that the Germans had considered doomed to extinction.

During one of his first exploratory walks into town, while testing his freedom Eddy had already abandoned his concrete-bag undershirt and had obtained a small valise. Most waited quietly much the same as they had before liberation, not having anything pressing or anywhere to go. Slowly, the numbers in camp became smaller.

***

Eddy spent several more days inside his old barracks, recovering at Ebensee in Austria.

Ode to Life!

After slowly adding real sustenance to his diet, and when the Americans were sure that everyone was able to tolerate real food, soups, vegetables, dumplings, SPAM, K-Rations etc were added. If one of the liberated was very weak they took them right away to field hospitals nearby.

The American military, 3rd Army was in charge of processing everyone. Logistics took time, so without being asked everyone stayed in their barracks until arrangements to go to different barracks in Linz (a town on the edge of the Danube) could be made. Further arrangements were then made to allow Eddy to return to Prague.

Eddy almost could not remember his last normal ride inside the passenger car of a train. Seated with other former prisoners, still in prison garb, and those who were regular travelers, he fell asleep. When he awoke and got off the train, it was nighttime. He stood only a moment at the station which made him a little uneasy.

Shortly out of town, Eddy found a small area under a bridge and went to sleep. Again he found comfort in the oblivion of slumber, though this trip was quite different than anything he'd experienced since living with his family.

What travelers found now were makeshift kitchens at almost every stop and local people, not the former Nazis, sharing supplies and cooking meals at every station. Perhaps, beyond what was felt in America during the Great Depression, people banded together, gave what they could and helped one another.

When Eddy awoke he felt a new sense of pursuit driving him. Eddy's current quest was to try and find out if his brother Karl had survived and he felt that Prague was a likely drop off point if that were the case. Sadly, with days of considerable effort, he found no evidence that any member of his family had survived. He then took a train to Budapest as he had been told of a sighting of his brother. Eddy stayed hopeful for about a week more, but without success.

***

Afterward Eddy made his way home to the town where he had grown up. He wanted to see if he could find *anyone* from his former life who might be still be alive. Maybe, his brother *was* alive, and he'd find him there. When Eddy arrived in his hometown, he walked towards his home where he ran into the town's mayor, who had been a close friend of Eddy's father who had been the head of the communist party there.

"What are your plans?"

"I'm going to see the old house," Eddy responded.

The mayor said, "After you do that, you are going to come and stay with me for awhile. My wife and I will take care of you. You can find work and get your bearings."

Eddy did not argue. From there, Eddy went to visit the place where he'd grown up and where he'd honed the many skills he used to survive his enslavement.

Ode to Life!

It was a short but memory-filled walk to the old Hoffman house. He recognized every fence post and tree and the dirt road seemed to buoy him up.

When he arrived at the front door it was still locked, but Eddy knew where an extra key had been placed. He lifted a loose board in the porch and almost amazed, found the key there. He entered and stood in the open doorway for only a moment before deciding that he had seen enough and that this quest was over. He could not stay in this house anymore. What would be the point of staying in his old home? Eddy didn't know, but being there for only a moment stirred such a deep sadness in Eddy that he knew he would never be able to stay there any longer, let alone live there ever again. He turned and walked away at a measured pace, returning the key to where he'd found it. Maybe some other lucky family member would come back and take his place as master of the manor.

***

Eddy took the mayor up on his offer, staying there for a short time. He went to work everyday doing this and that. In the country at the time it really didn't matter what you did because you got paid the same amount every day. That's how communism works.

On Friday's all workers got a little money in a bag, a bar of chocolate and a liter of vodka. Eventually the mayor gave money and documents to Eddy so that he could attend college in Kiev, the capitol of Ukraine. Eddy took the money, but Eddy didn't want to be in the area anymore, or to become a Russian citizen. Eddy knew that if he stayed in the area he would be old enough soon to join the military.

The mayor and police chief had spoken to Eddy about this commitment, saying that Eddy, "Had what it took," to become a Russian officer.

What really tipped the scales against the Communist system for Eddy was when he went to a wedding just prior to this, and a Russian soldier who was drunk was playing with his knife. Tossing his knife again and again without anyone commenting until one throw took one of the fingers of the groom.

A Russian Cossack Officer yelled at his subordinate,"Hey, you can't be doing things like this! You're making the whole Russian Army look bad."

At that, without emotion, the Cossack Officer took out his side arm pistol aimed and shot the subordinate soldier squarely through the heart. The soldier fell to the floor in front of the wedding table where the groom was still hollering from losing his finger. No one responded to the killing of the Russian, and that was enough to keep Eddy as far away from Russians as he could get.

***

When the Germans left and the Russians took control of the land, Eddy didn't like their form of government. It was communist and a very strong dictatorship. All traces of Nazis occupation were being erased, however. Soon, it was as if the Nazis never existed. In addition, Eddy knew that

Ode to Life!

the Russians were in the habit of kidnapping men off of the street and constricting them into their military.

***

Eddy knew that he wanted to get away, because there had to be something better. He felt, probably due to his parents' and grandparents preconceptions that the Russians were primitive people, that Russia was not a good option. Eddy was seeking sophistication.

He decided to head for his cousins in Northern Czechoslovakia. They had a nice apartment and Eddy would have a place to crash for awhile. He would have his own room. In Prague, they had an organization, the American Jewish Joint Distribution service, and they had a huge home for kids aged under 16 he had heard about.

Eddy went to Prague and found the orphanage. He stayed there for awhile. They fed him breakfast, lunch and dinner. The orphanage was paid for by the Americans. In January 1945, the Jewish Agency organized those who were under 16 to go to Great Britain. There were over 720 orphans. Then 49 of those children were sent to Northern Ireland which included Eddy. They fixed Eddy's papers so that it looked like he was under 16 since he had just turned 16.

Of the forty-nine kids who were flown to Northern Ireland, there were twenty-four girls and twenty-five boys. Everyone of them were orphans from the war. They were being put onto an American Military plane. This was

January 1946. From then on there was always forty-nine children, because one girl didn't make the Prague flight.

The first time Eddy had been on a plane, it was a single engine, four wing plane. He was about nine years old. It was 1938 during a flying exhibition that had been set up for the school kids outside Eddy's town. His father had many important friends, so somehow got permission to have Eddy participate.

This, Eddy's second flight was going to take him to the orphanage. He was amazed when he saw the ocean from the air. He had never seen so much water. The flight was from Prague to Belfast. The children received small packages upon landing, filled with chocolate and sweets of assorted kinds. They also gave the children tea with milk which, before this Eddy thought only sick people drank.

The children were told not to discuss what was happening among themselves or talk to anyone, because they were not supposed to fly out of Prague without papers ,which they didn't have. So in case they were questioned, they were instructed to say only that they were being flown around the city to show them the sights in the area. Eddy /noticed there were a lot of secret police around, and this level of attention helped him see a sign when he boarded that read, "No Smoking."

Eddy thought that meant no smoking jacket for some reason, which to him meant that no one should wear a black tail jacket.

He was relieved since he thought,"I don't have to worry cause I don't have one of those!"

When the children arrived in Ireland, not a single one of them could speak English. At the time Eddy knew Hungarian, Yiddish, German and a little Russian and Polish.

Everyone was put onto classic red double decker buses to Millisle. The buses were headed right to the barracks where everyone was going to sleep, but the bus was too heavy for the soggy roads, and got stuck in the mud! All the boys had to get out and push the bus, until it was pushed from the ditches that the wheels had dug. When they arrived to the barracks they received Cadbury Chocolate and their own toiletries, which was another great new gift of freedom, as far as Eddy was concerned.

***

They put everyone on a Farm in Northern Island for ten months. Kids had been shipped all over Western Europe. Over time, seven-hundred and twenty children were sent to Great Britain. For years Eddy had been shipped all over the place as a slave, but when these children made it to Britain, it was wonderful in his mind.

He had learned to speak English while in Northern Ireland. They had good teachers. English was difficult as nothing sounds like it is spelled, but Eddy's teachers were excellent and the orphans all learned quickly. One of the professors was Dr. Weiner. He had previously been Dean of a university in Austria, escaping before the war. He was now in charge of the schooling for the children.

Eddy really learned the language by walking with this professor everyday and studying from the Germain/English Dictionary. Eddy tried, and succeeded to pick up five or ten new words every day.

***

After ten months they closed the farm and moved the Orphans to Manchester, an area called Burnley. There were another forty to fifty kids there who had also been orphaned.

Eventually Eddy found a job in Glasgow, Scotland. There was another orphanage in that area and Eddy was able to get work at a hotel there. Eddy worked there for awhile, accumulated some money and then moved to London.

Eddy went to London by himself and found another orphanage that would house him. Eventually Eddy found a job in a German style bakery. Eddy wasn't paid much, but it was enough to rent a room with a Jewish friend named Jules Blum who he had met in the orphanage. Jules became a jeweler and they lived together in the Jewelry section of Glasgow for a while, until Eddy decided to move to London. When he did move, it was solo.

When he got settled in London Eddy called Jules and told him, "Hey Jules, come on down and I'll talk to my landlady about you staying with me." Jules came down and they shared a room, and Jules got another job working in the jewelry business.

Even though they were living in the section of London where jewelers abounded, Eddy continued in the bakery. However, it was hard to save money on what he was making. Insurance cost three pounds, a suit was more than twenty pounds and everything else seemed very expensive, as well.

One day Eddy decided to go to Petticoat Lane to walk around and while there he thought to himself, "I think I'm going to work here."

So Eddy went to a company where they made plastic beads for cheap jewelry, found out who was in charge and told the boss that he wanted to sell his product on Petticoat Lane. Eddy said he would sell the merchandise, but for now all Eddy had was a bicycle. "I don't have any money to get started, I will leave my bike as collateral."

That's how Eddy started in business. He knew he needed a product, but he didn't have any funds.

The boss agreed to give Eddy a whole box of beads. He then looked at Eddy and said, "Go ahead, take the bike. I know you'll come back and pay me soon, and I really don't want to be responsible for your bike."

Eddy got the deal and was in business for himself.

At 4 a.m. Eddy set up a little box on the street and put a piece of cloth over it. Eddy wasn't there but a few minutes when a policeman came and said Eddy had to buy a daily permit. Eddy said to the policeman, "Do me a favor, go the other way and come back, and then I'll buy it when you come back." So he looked at me, agreed and left. By the time he came back, Eddy had sold all the pop beads. A lot of women liked them Eddy mused. His mind did little wandering but he was content, as he continued sitting there waiting for the policeman to come back. Eddy wanted to make sure he kept his promise.

The Policeman was amazed that Eddy had waited for him. Eddy thought he appreciated it. He made more money there then all week long at the bakery. So Eddy went out there quite a few times. He made some money then he decided to do some more baking.

***

Eddy spoke with his landlady and was able to get a permit to open a catering business. He had the idea to cater clubs all over London and to sell them food late at night. So, Eddy bought an old Ford Van and went to the nightclubs telling the owners, "I'll bring you some items everyday. What you don't sell, I'll take back; so what can you lose?"

This sounded like a good idea to the nightclub owners. So Eddy got his first order, then more and more of them, cutting corners by delivering the goods himself.

***

In the meantime Eddy went in with a Polish guy who was experienced with all things business and said "Look, you and me, we know the trade. I know some things but not everything and we will share the profits, alright?"

Within the first week they were pulling in between 20 and 22 pounds a week, each. That was working from 5 to 8 at night. So he was a good worker. The only problem Eddy had with him is that he was married and had a kid and didn't want to work extra or at night. During Christmas time Eddy couldn't go home to take a bath or shower and was so busy he had to go in the back of work just to snooze a little and go back to work. Eddy worked day and night. At Christmas time sometimes three days where Eddy didn't go home. He was 18 at the time.

Eddy told him, "I don't mind sharing the profits but after all, you have to put in the time like I do.

He said, "Eddy I'm married and have a kid! You are single! You can do what you want, when you want."

"Well, all right," Eddy thought.

He worked the bakery for a couple of years and eventually sold it. He didn't even ask his partner. After all, Eddy had done all the work and had to make all the decisions. Eddy had been waiting to receive papers from the American Council. He wanted to go to the United States and visit his cousins who were living in Cleveland. In 1951 the papers came. Ed was 22.

***

Before leaving, while still living in London, Eddy was looking for a friend but couldn't find the street on the address he had written. He noticed a couple who were doing some gardening, and asked for directions. The man said his name was Nifeld Bela (an accent on the e). Eddy was surprised because he recognized the name. This was the same man that he had known while still living at home. Eddy asked if he was related to a guy he used to know.

The man said "That's me!"

After getting reacquainted Nifeld said, "Come over for dinner," and that started a ritual of at least twice a week. Nifeld liked to give Eddy advice about life. He advised Eddy (among other things) to find a wife. After six months Eddy told him he was finally going to America.

Until that time, Nifeld had never mentioned that he had a brother in Long Island and that the brother had passed away. So, when Eddy was ready to leave, Nifeld and his wife took him to the train station. His wife, Rosy baked and roasted a duck for Eddy's journey so the young world traveler wouldn't get hungry. On the way to the train station, Nifeld started telling Eddy about his brother.

The brother had property in Long Island. He also had owned a car and had a hefty bank account which Nifeld had inherited with his brother's passing. He wanted Eddy to have everything his brother had left. Apparently Rosy and Nifeld had planned the whole thing out. They knew they would never go to America, but didn't want the property to go to waste.

He even gave Eddy an introduction letter for his brother's attorney. He said to have the attorney in the States call him to verify that he wanted Eddy to have all of his deceased brother's property, car, and bank account included.

Ode to Life!

This bothered Eddy to no end, but took the letter and the Duck and said goodbye. He gave the whole thing a lot of thought, and when Eddy got to the U.S. he decided not to contact the attorney. Instead, he wrote to Nifeld and thanked him for his generosity, but said he couldn't go through with it.

Until this time it was unclear if anyone knew Eddy was alive and Ed didn't really know exactly where (if any of) his relatives might living. He decided to go anyway. After selling his business Eddy went down to Piccadilly Circus.

While walking around he came upon a travel agency with lots of posters on ships, and he thought, "You know, I have papers to go to The States, so I might as well try to go there.." Eddy walked into the shipping office and asked if they had any openings on the ship. "Oh yes we do!" was the swift answer.

***

Sure enough they had a room on the SS America. It was a luxury liner, not a cheap one. It was a sleek vessel with the look of a cruise liner, but a little smaller. So Eddy said, "O.k. I'll buy the ticket." It was a one way ticket. Eddy was not looking backward.

***

In the meantime he already had the English Passport, at that time, so he decided to come to the United States with the Passport. So Eddy finally got to New York. It was not smooth sailing; Eddy was sick the entire way as the Atlantic was extremely rough especially in January and

February. Memories of the sickness that prisoners had experienced in the previous Christmas, while Eddy was held in slavery, flashed into his mind.

He was sick as a dog, but didn't want to give in to something as simple as a wavy ocean, so everyday he used to go into the pool and would stay in the pool and float with the water, This seemed to make him feel better. It took five days to get across the Atlantic. Eddy met a woman at his table the first night but was so sick, he could not come to the dining room after that. She was from France. She would come down to Eddy's cabin and bring him food.

She then decided to stay and take *care* of Eddy.

When they got to New York, she told him not to mention that little fact to her husband, "In fact," she said. "It is best we just act like we don't know each other at all."

Her husband was meeting her at the dock, and he was an Army officer.

***

When Eddy arrived into New York Harbor, he smiled from ear to ear and said to himself, "Boy this is a wonderful country."

From New York, Eddy decided to go to Cleveland, Ohio. Eddy knew all his cousins were there. He arrived in Cleveland on a Sunday morning. His cousin Joe Hoffman had already found Eddy a job with a wholesale bakery.

So, on Monday morning Eddy had a job. It was February 1952.

Right away Eddy signed with a union and Eddy's wages were $96 a week, about $19 a day. It was wonderful because Eddy could go out and buy himself with a week's wages a suit, a shirt, shoes, underwear, everything that was needed for a complete wardrobe. Shortly after, working at the bakery, he was put in charge of his department which included about 20 employees. Eddy guessed they saw he could do more than the basic work.

***

Eddy and his friend Spiegel were together from Auschwitz onward and they reconnected at the orphanage in Prague.

Ignac Deutsch and Jan Czuker were there as well as many other friends.

He made it to what was northern Czechoslovakia and found his *cousins* there (first cousins on father side) Joe Hoffman, Perry, Toby, Bela children of Ed's father's brother Simcha...the same uncle who was in Auschwitz and stayed behind with Eddy's brother. He had actually met Joe Hoffman on the train from Bucharest, 300 kilometers away from Eddy's home town.

***

Circumstances for every orphan was different, coming from all over Europe, different camps. It took a few days for more of the Hoffman clan to come together. Family members (those related to Eddy's mother) did not show up because none had survived.

Eddy's cousins had a nice apartment in Northern Czechoslovakia and offered Eddy a place to stay for as long as he needed. He had his own room and was comfortable, All the survivors were given keys to the apartments and businesses which had belonged to the German people before and during the war. The Chech government kicked out all the Germans living there. Eddy still wanted to travel to Prague.

In Prague, there was a huge home for kids age 15-18. Eddy went there and stayed for awhile. They fed the teens breakfast, lunch and dinner. It was paid for by Americans. JEWISH AMERICAN JOINT DISTRIBUTION (JOINT).

***

Everyone of them were orphans from the war. When they arrived in Ireland, not a single one (including Eddy) could speak English. At the time Eddy spoke Hungarian, Yiddish, German and little Chech, Russian and Polish.

They put 49 kids on a Farm called Millisle in Northern Ireland for 10 months. Here he met Jan again. This was the nephew of Adolph Zukor, a movie producer of some later repute, having produced (among other things) a famous Betty Boop cartoon and other films.

***

There was a girl named Pery, another orphan who had had come from a village very close to where Eddy had come from. Pery had an older sister who was also orphaned because of the war.

Ode to Life!

For some reason, Pery was very attracted to Eddy. Eddy always seemed to be of interest to the young women. At night Pery would come to his window to give him flowers. This happened day after day from the second day they were in the orphanage. Pery would get up extra early and pick flowers and put them on Eddy's window sill. She also knitted Eddy socks and a scarf. Eddy was not playing hard to get, he spent a lot of time with Pery and they became close. She gave Eddy a silver cigarette case that she purchased with money that was sent by relatives in New York. She paid for his movie tickets and bus fare into town to see the movies in Dunagan Dee.

***

Orphans had been shipped all over western Europe. In fact 720 children including Eddy were sent to Great Britain. From there the British Jewish organization took over and signed everyone up in the government. For years Eddy got used to being shipped, marched, transported all over the place, but when he made it to Britain he felt it was wonderful.

While on the farm they also worked. The farm had potatoes, chickens and other vegetables. It was like having a large family again for Eddy. Many of them were from the Carpathian Mountains and many of them became very successful in their work in America. Some stayed in London and never came to America. Every five years they would have a reunion in London.

***

***

He was in London when Gandhi was killed and when Israel became a state.

Eddy would go to Hyde Park to hear political speeches whenever he had a few extra hours.

The first written record of Jewish settlement in England dates back 1070 to the reign of William the Conqueror.

A Jewish settlement flourished until King Edward I, in his *Edict of Expulsion* in 1290. After this expulsion, there was no overt Jewish community in England, but individuals practiced Judaism secretly in the mid-1600s during the rule of Oliver Cromwell. While Cromwell never officially readmitted Jews to the Commonwealth of England, a small colony of Sephardic Jews living in London were allowed to remain.

In 1753 the *Jewish Naturalization Act* attempted to legalize Jewish presence in England, but this normalization only lasted for a few months.

1846 the British law "De Judaismo" prescribed a special dress for Jews, was later repealed, and then things began to improve. When Benjamin Disraeli, born Jewish but converted to Anglicanism, was elected twice as the Prime Minister of the United Kingdom in 1868 and in 1874 there was a little bit of soul searching taking place in theU.K.

Due to the lack of anti-Jewish violence in Britain in the 19th century, it acquired a reputation for religious tolerance and attracted significant immigration from Eastern Europe.

In the 1930s and 1940s, some European Jews fled to England to escape the Nazis.

Jews faced antisemitism and stereotyping in Britain after WWII, because Jews were equated with Germans in the early 20th century, despite the fact that the English themselves had partial Germanic ethnic origins. This led many Ashkenazi Jewish families to Anglicize their often German-sounding names, and change spellings of names (such as Karl to Carl, or Josef to Joseph) to blend in better.

***

England now contains the second largest Jewish population in Europe (behind France) and the fifth largest Jewish community worldwide. The majority of the Jews in England live in and around London.

On the other hand, London was the number one target of the Blitzkrieg Bombings or the Blitz throughout the war. These were terrifying nighttime bombing raids against London and other British cities by Nazi Germany which kept about 1/2 of all residents away from their homes for all or part of the war effort.

Evidence of the bombings wasn't too bad in 1948. A few buildings were collapsed. There had been too many RAF planes to make air attacks worthwhile. The French and Polish pilots had been launching from North of London, toward Manchester.

***

Eddy had lived under all kinds of rule: communist, capitalist, monarchy, democratic, socialist and was open to hearing how each might improve the lives of the average person, as he felt he was.

***

One day, while Eddy was listening to a political speech word came of the assassination of Gandhi.

In Hyde Park, every weekend, any speaker was allowed to speak on any subject as long as you didn't insult the King and Queen.

Hyde Park was also known as Marble Arch Corner.

Eddy didn't have much knowledge about Gandhi.

Britain was loosing Egyptian influence.

You could be anti-*anything*, but Eddy didn't feel anti-semitism at all.

Before Israel became a country Turkey had all the control in the area, and they were all Arab.

Britain was very involved with Arab countries because of their interest in Arab oil. The Arabs controlled much of North Africa. Because Arabs were anti-Jewish, Britain had no choice but to be anti-Jewish also, they thought.

***

"All right, thanks." So, just like that, Eddy created another job for himself.

Edd spoke with his landlady and was able to get a permit to open a catering business. He had the idea to cater clubs all over London and to sell them food late afternoon. The government did not ration businesses, only individuals. By now he had earned enough and bought an old Ford Van, which he drove to the nightclubs nearby. He told the owners and managers of the clubs," Could you please take some of my pastries and finger sandwiches to sell in your club? You can sell them for a reasonable amount and I'll take a percentage. What you don't sell, I will take back! So what can you lose?"

This was an easy way to make more money without any effort for the clubs. So Eddy got orders, more and more of them. And he delivered the goods himself. In meantime he went in with a Polish guy who was an experienced baker and said "Look, you and me, you know the trade well, I know some things but not everything, and we will share the profits, alright?"

Within the first week we were pulling between 20 and 22 pounds a week between each of us. That was working from 5 in the morning to 8 at night. The Polish guy was a good worker. The only problem Ed had with him, was that this guy was married and had a kid and didn't want to work extra at night, or during Christmas time, so Eddy picked up the slack and even pulled a three nighter more often than not. He couldn't even go home to take a bath or shower and was so busy he would just snooze a little in a chair and go back to work. He was nineteen years old at the time.

***

Eddy decided to talk to his Polish worker "You know, I don't mind sharing the profits but after all, you have to put in the time like I do."

He said, "I am married, I have a kid!! You are single! You can do what you want!"

Eddy said "Well, what's one thing got to do with the other"?

So Eddy worked the bakery for a couple of years and eventually he sold it off. Besides owning everything, Eddy had done all the work. He had been waiting to receive papers from the American Council. He wanted to go to the United States and visit his cousins in Cleveland and his two uncles who were living in Philadelphia. In 1951 the papers came. Eddy Hoffman, formerly Adolf Hoffman, aka Bumi was just 21 years of age.

After selling his business he went down to Picadilly Circus by the waterfront. Eddy was walking around and came to the side of a large shipping office and thought, "You know, I have papers to go to the states. I might as well try it."

Eddy walked in and asked if they have any openings on the ship.

"Oh yes we do!"

Sure enough they had a room on the SS America. It was a luxury liner, not a cheap liner. Like a cruise liner, but a little smaller.

So Eddy said, "Ok I'll buy the ticket."

It was a one way ticket to America. Eddy had an English Passport at that time, so he decided to come to the United States and arrived in New York.

The journey was difficult for Eddy. He was sick the entire way as the Atlantic was extremely rough especially in January and February. Eddy was sick as a dog, so everyday he went into the pool and would stay in the pool all day and would float with the water so he would feel better. It took five or six days to get across the Atlantic. While on board, Eddy met a woman at his dining room table the first night, but he was so sick he could not go to the dining room after that. This woman was from France. She would come down to his cabin and bring Eddy food. She then decided to stay in his room and take care of him. When they got to New York, she told him not to mention to anyone that she had cared for him or even that he knew her. At the gang-plank the woman met her husband. Eddy saw the two embrace. The husband was an Army officer. Until then Eddy had no idea that she was married. He walked by without even a gesture.

***

When Eddy arrived in New York on the weekend, he said--as he did when he arrived in Britain, "Boy this is a wonderful country." He enjoyed walking the streets and noticing all the businesses, especially the food operations. All the hustle and bustle really appealed to him. He immediately walked to the Pennsylvania Station at 29th Street and 7th Avenue. He bought himself a ticket to Cleveland, Ohio. He slept on a bench inside the station until the train arrived in the middle of the night. He arrived in Cleveland the next morning on Sunday. His cousin Joe Hoffman was waiting for him when he arrived. Joe had already found his cousin Eddy a job with a wholesale bakery. So, on Monday morning he started his new job. It was February 1952.

Right away Ed signed with a union and his wages were $96 a week, about $20 a day. It was wonderful because he could go out and buy himself, with a week's wages, a suit, a shirt, shoes, underwear, everything. So he started working with that company. They made him a foreman of the department he worked in. Eddy guessed they saw he could do more than the basic work.

Five months later, thanks to the United States Military, everything changed again for Eddy, but somehow he managed to stay exactly the same as he had always been.

Ode to Life!

as told to Gordon Richiusa

Chapter Eight
Hoffman Was Here

When he arrived in the U.S., he had to register for the draft and sure enough his name was picked. He had basic training in Breckenridge Kentucky with the 101st Airborne. This fort was named after the 14th VP of the United States.

Over the years Eddy was spelled many ways, with some insisting on calling him Ed or Edward, but Eddy knew who he was and the name or the spelling didn't matter. Eddy's name was still technically Adolf. He had, however not used that name since his enlistment in the U.S. Military. It was noted by the recruitment officer that Adolf Hoffman and Adolf Hitler not only had the same initials but the same first names. Eddy decided that *Adolf* Hoffman would have a better time of life if everyone simply started calling him Eddy. This change was encouraged by the U.S. Military.

***

So, five months after he emigrated to the U.S. Eddy got drafted into the Korean War. When Eddy had arrived in the U.S., he was told he had to register for the draft, which he was happy to do, since he felt that Patton's army had liberated him. Sure enough, right away Eddy's name was picked.

Ode to Life!

He would go to basic training in Breckenridge Kentucky with 101 Airborne. Eddy was just getting comfortable with having control over his own life, so when he arrived in Kentucky it was so cold there that Eddy was not happy. He really wanted to be out of the cold so Eddy asked his Captain, "Sir, do you need a baker for the company?"

"Yeah, do you know one?"

Eddy said, "Yeah, me." He got the job.

***

They had about 220 people in the company, and because Eddy was the baker he was given a special room away from the regular barracks. Eddy could sleep later than some of the others and didn't have to wake up with everyone else. After breakfast, all the soldiers went out onto the field to train. but Eddy slept on and went in and took over the kitchen around 11:00 a.m. to do the baking for the next 24 hours, which only took Eddy about 4 to 5 hours. After which he had the entire rest of the day to himself to go to a movie or the PX. Eddy would check out some of the other kitchens after he returned from the movies around 8 or 9 in the evenings and see how the other bakers were still struggling to finish the 24 hour baking.

The captain gave orders to the other cooks to give Eddy room to do what everyone felt was a very important job. They were all cooks, but Eddy was the baker. So he started baking whatever was on the menu. From that day on, many officers from different companies came to have breakfast there because they really liked Eddy's baking.

One guy, John J. Hanna was in charge of the kitchen, but was told specifically, "You are NOT in charge of the baker." This did not seem to bother John J. In fact, he and Eddy became friends. John had a Pontiac and would often drive Eddy back and forth from Pennsylvania (where John J.'s family lived) to Cleveland (which Eddy felt was his home) and back to Camp. One trip he invited Eddy to come to his house and share a Christmas dinner. Eddy was not particularly fond of this or any other holiday, but he loved home cooked meals.

When they arrived at the Hanna home, they were greeted by several family members, including one uncle who was a Greek Orthodox Catholic priest.

When Eddy saw the big headpiece on top of the uncle's head, he knew he was a priest, and for some reason Eddy greeted him with the Arab expression, "As-Salaam 'alaykum," which means *Peace be upon you*.

This set off a nearly non-stop barrage of Arabic from the priest/uncle, which lasted long into the night. When John J. and Eddy were leaving, the priest/uncle took Eddy's head in both his hands, bowed his head and said what Eddy believed was a special prayer.

On the drive home John J. said to Eddy, "I didn't know you spoke Arabic."

"I don't," Eddy responded with a smile. "Those were the only Arabic words I know. They just came out of my mouth!"

Eddy spent the whole basic training in the kitchen. The day Eddy was supposed to graduate basic training the captain came in and said, "Eddy I can't sign you off on basic training, because you never went out into the field."

Eddy asked, "So what now?"

The captain shuffled around some papers and manuals he was carrying around with him, without really reading anything and finally said, "You know what? Put on your jacket and let's go right now and get you qualified!"

They went immediately to the practice field, from one station to the next to the next.

The captain said, "Here's a rifle. See that target?"

"Sure."

"Okay then, shoot."

Eddy would shoot.

"Good, you passed!"

Then, "Do this--you passed. Do that--you passed," and so on until he was able to sign Eddy off on all basic training requirements.

***

When anyone was drafted they were given a series of placement exams. So, after qualifying the captain took a look at Eddy's exam scores and said, "You know Eddy, I think you'd be alright as an officer."

The two of them went out into the parade area. There were tables set up when scorekeepers and others checking documents. The captain said, "Now, go over to that table over there." He pointed. "Tell them I sent you to start OCS (Officers Candidate School)."

Eddy did as directed, went to the OCS table, sat down there. There was no one else waiting that he could see, but suddenly, without looking up, a voice came from the clerk.

"Name?"

"Hoffman."

"Do you have any paperwork?"

Eddy handed what he had. They looked at the scores from basic training and the handwritten recommendation from the captain.

"You're an American, yes?" OCS clerk led with this question.

Eddy hesitated, then responded, "Wait a minute, hold it."

"Well, Hoffman is an American name, right?" He was asked again.

Eddy said, "What do you mean I'm American? I just came to this country?"

"Then what the hell are you doing here?"

Eddy said, "Look, I was drafted and sent by the captain."

"Okay," the guy at the table said. "You have two choices. The first is you can be a private, or if you pass the language test--and with three languages that shouldn't be a problem--then you can join the military intelligence school. It also says here that you are a first class baker. So, you could go to Chicago and teach baking for the military."

Eddy was sure that the captain wanted him to remain a baker, but knew that he probably would be baking the rest of his life. He wanted to experience new things."Let me think about it a minute." He did not take the whole minute to decide. "I'll go to military intelligence school," Eddy told the clerk.

They sent him to Fort Jackson first, and from there to Fort Bragg in North Carolina, 3rd Army, and Eddy ended up in MIS, OB which is Military Intelligence and Order of Battle. It was the same Company which had liberated him. It was also a base that was named after a Confederate General. Eddy did not know much about the U.S. Civil War at the time, so the name meant little to him.

At the same time, his friend in the kitchen, John J. Hanna was sent to Korea into combat. Eddy later heard that John J. was killed in action there.

***

After Eddy was sent to Fort Bragg, North Carolina for military Intelligence. Eddy went to visit the nearby town of Fayetteville and noticed something that shook him to the core. Before he found his way to his first assignment, he needed to use the latrine, asking a passing soldier, "Where is the latrine?"

The soldier politely pointed Eddy in the right direction, to a building, something like an old west saloon with two doors, separated by about twenty five feet of space.

Above one door was the word: WHITE.

Above the other door was the word: BLACK.

The two doorways to separate latrines immediately sparked rebellion in Eddy's heart. He couldn't understand why the people who had rescued him from the Nazis' blind prejudice which had allowed the elimination of every member of his immediate family, would openly condone racial discrimination against people who were actively engaged in protecting the freedoms of his adopted country.

Without hesitation, Eddy walked through the door marked: BLACK. No one looked at him or said a word about this choice. When he was finished, he began his basic training.

***

Eddy was in military intelligence school for quite awhile. While he was there Eddy had a girlfriend in Cleveland. He wasn't that into the relationship though. At one point the girl said, "I'm coming out to see you." Eddy was over it though and said, "I'm being shipped out," which wasn't, as yet, true.

So, that day Eddy went to the company commander and said, "Do me a favor, send me over seas."

"Are you crazy? What for?"

"Look I've got my reasons."

Ode to Life!

Eddy thought he needed to get away! Being sent overseas for a year would be just enough.

Eddy added, "If you could do me another favor, and please don't send me to Europe. I've been to Europe. I'm from Europe. But, I've never been to the Far East. Please send me there." He reasoned that this might be the only way he'd ever get to see the Asian continent. "I don't care if its Korea or Japan," he said. "Please just send me over there."

Luckily, the commander decided to send Eddy to Japan. Eddy was 23 years old.

***

Eddy made ready to sail right away out of a port called Pittsburg California, just outside of San Francisco. There was a big camp there, but they put several on a military ship destined for Japan.

When they were just about to set sail, Eddy stood on deck, leaning against the railing. Next to him was another American soldier. As the ship started to slowly get underway and pass under a bridge, Eddy watched as this guy climbed up over the railing and dove into the ocean!

Eddy was shocked that this guy had jumped right into water and started swimming toward shore. Right away a helicopter was deployed from somewhere and waited for him on the shore. When he got there, they picked him up and brought him back onto the ship.

***

The Navy Captain came to Eddy and said "You were standing next to him; you saw him jump?"

Eddy responded immediately, but with calm, "Captain, I really couldn't tell you anything about it, to tell the truth."

"Why?"

"Because I was turning my back to the guy."

Eddy didn't want to get into trouble or cause any trouble for any other soldier. The guy who had jumped and quickly returned claimed he had fallen off the deck!

Eddy continued, "By the time I heard a big plop, he was in the water."

The captain said, "Okay." Then he added, "You know Hoffman, you want a good job?"

Eddy said, "Sure."

He looked at Eddy, "You go down one floor and go to the PX and tell the officer in charge that the Captain sent you."

Eddy did what he was told. The officer in question who was sitting behind a big desk looked at Eddy and gave him a big stack of all kinds of papers. Then he said, "I want you to be at the military PX store every morning from 10 am. to 12 p.m." After that time, all the enlisted men could enter the store.

"What's my assignment?"

"You stand out front of the company store. You aren't allowed to let any enlisted men enter, only officers and NCO's."

So Eddy said, "Fine," and was given the job.

Ode to Life!

Eddy went back to his cabin. There were a lot of guys there. The Master Sargent who was in charge of the cabin made a statement to all these guys. This cabin will be pulling KP duty for the entire two week trip (Kitchen Police, like pots and pans.) Eddy told the Master Sargent "I was assigned to be an M.P. I got this job watching over the store." What a great assignment. He was able to go for his meals any time he desired and always able to move right to the front of the line.

***

Every morning Eddy made sure the officers were in line. At the same time, as another perk, Eddy could buy anything he wanted, which he did near the end of his shift.

This seemed like it had great potential to Eddy who decided to go back to his roots and buy boxes of chocolates, candy, cards, and a variety of stuff that he could sell to those who could not get into the line.

At the end of every shift, Eddy took what he'd purchased upstairs to where the enlisted men were concentrated and sold the candy at a quarter a bar, and the other items at prices and in quantities that the enlisted were happy to pay. Then after 12:00 pm the lines waiting to get into the store were impossible. So, if Eddy hadn't done this, none of them would have access to any of these goods. By the time Eddy got to Japan he had about $700 profit over what his pay would have been. When he finished selling all he had, which was easy and only took a half hour, he spent the rest of the day sun bathing.

as told to Gordon Richiusa

***

The trip took two weeks. Eddy ended up in Okinawa which is eastern Japan, near Tokyo. His whole group was assigned as ski troopers and worked in very heavy snow. Eddy had never skied before but he and the other troopers were given full equipment and required to participate in daily ski exercises, as well as maintain their equipment in typical Army fashion. The skis issued were really long wooden ones, and each night each trooper had to scrape and wax their own skis. This whole Ski Patrol was only there as a precaution in case the Russians might decide to come around. It was during the outset of the Cold War.

***

Eddy's tour lasted two years. That was standard for the draft during the Korean War. In fact, Eddy always thought that a draft was a good idea, but he was looking at it from possibly a unique perspective. Eddy liked the military. He thought service straightens a person up and teaches them to be organized. The service also helped one become disciplined and emphasized not only physical but mental toughness.

***

In Fort Bragg NC when Eddy was in the 82nd airborne, Eddy got friendly with Captain Jack Hemingway, Ernest Hemingways eldest son, he was Eddy's captain. He'd say, "Hey Hoffman, let's go fishin'. I'll buy you a big breakfast."

"Thank you but no."

"Hoffman, it's an order," Jack Hemingway would say, and Eddy would have to go.

He used to call Eddy up and even though Eddy had a girlfriend and Hemingway had a wife, the captain just wanted to have some fun. He'd call and say, "Hey Hoffman, put on some civilian clothes. Let's go to a concert, or the officers club, have a few drinks." The Captain had fixed Eddy up with a General's secretary and told Eddy to bring her along.

He told Eddy to wear his civilian clothes because if he had his uniform on they wouldn't let him into the officer's club. Eddy was worried at first, but realized that he was sort of immune from military retribution, since he was with a Captain and just following orders. Also, Eddy and Jack Hemingway got along very well. So, it wasn't much of a problem to spend time with the Caption. Captain Hemingway said to Eddy, "Can you promise me that when you get discharged, you will call me? You and me will go into business together." Eddy replied, "I appreciate your offer, and I'll think about it.", but didn't bother to look up his commanding officer when Eddy got discharged. Eddy thought to himself, "Why do I need him as a partner?" The Captain lived in his late father's home in Florida.

**

Eddy was always getting special treatment. He didn't know why or really care. He took everything in stride. That is one of the characteristics which attracted Eveline. Eddy always made her feel safe and could manage any new situation that life threw their way.

One day Eddy received an order saying that he was being shipped back to Tokyo to get discharged. He knew that meant that he'd soon be sent back to the United States. Eddy was supposed to take the train and then the boat on Wednesday morning all the way to Tokyo. But then orders got changed for them to leave earlier on Monday morning. The soldiers exited the train and boarded the boat. Then the train drove up, inside, and onto the lower deck of the ship. When they crossed to Honshu, everyone debarked and waited to board the train to Tokyo, which took over a day to arrive.

It was the first time in years since WWII that the military changed the orders from shipping on Wednesday to shipping on Monday morning. That meant the soldiers had to get their gear right away and travel. By Wednesday they had made it to Tokyo.

That morning, on Wednesday, there was a news flash of a massive tsunami that had tipped the fleet ship upside down and drowned every soldier on it. That was the same ship that Eddy was supposed to travel on, but he had literally missed the boat. It was called The Tara Maru.

So Eddy got to Tokyo and was put on a ship in Yokohama outside Tokyo that's close to Mt. Fuji. The guy who was in charge of the 25 guys came in and called up names for all his company, so that they could be assigned to duties while aboard ship. About a dozen guys at a time got their work orders daily in this way, "You do this" and then twelve more guys "You do that." For some reason though Eddy and one other guy never had their names called. Eddy figured out what was going on, but did not say anything. He knew how these orders were printed and the Sgt. Major was only looking at one side of this assignment list. There were so many being shipped that Eddy and one other guy's name was on the other side of the paper.

So, after everyone else got their assignments, Eddy and the other soldier went upstairs and were sunbathing everyday, never once being called for duty.

After two weeks on the ship, they were near the Bay Bridge, and the Sgt. Major happened to be next to a sunbathing Eddy and his Italian buddy from New York. The Sgt. Major asked, "What unit are you with?"

Eddy said "What do you mean? I'm in your unit!"

"No way!" the Sgt. Major said.

"What do you mean 'No way?' I'm in your department sir." Eddy knew he could not directly contradict a superior.

"How come I didn't assign you to anything?"

"I don't know," Eddy said. "You never called my name when giving out assignments."

"What are you talking about? I called every name on my list! You're not on the list."

At that point he turned the list over and there were the two names which he'd never seen.

The Sgt. Major took a deep breath and walked away. The entire trip Eddy just got to kick back and relax! He never was given an assignment and apparently the Sergeant Major thought it better to forget it then admit he'd made a mistake.

***

Now, Eddy was free to do whatever he wanted, and in addition never saw any combat. However, they called Eddy a Korean War Veteran because he was in direct support of the troops. He had done important work, especially in the G2 department, which means military intelligence. They didn't have the G2 in Korea; they had it in Japan.

While in the military they'd tell Eddy what he had to do and he just followed orders. You can't question the military. In fact Eddy liked the military for that and other reasons, and while he served he found his allegiance to this adopted country was strengthened.

***

While in Tokyo, Ed and the rest of the Ski Patrol would go into town with some of his pals. One was a guy who really liked Asian women. Right before leaving the country, on one of these excursions, his friend was trying to get a good looking woman to join the three soldiers for a night on the town. The woman, however, did not have any interest in this guy. She immediately pointed at Eddy and said, "I'll go if HE is my date."

Eddy complied and the four of them became only two as Eddy was asked to take this woman home when the hour got late. He went into her home with her, then went back to base. He saw her again later a few times. Eddy thought the

Japanese women were beautiful, but he did not like the fishy oil smell that emanated from some of them. He was told that fish oil was used on their hair.

After three weeks in Tokyo, Eddy got orders to go to Sapporo, the capitol of Hokkaido with the 1st Calvary. He stayed there eight months working with military intelligence. Also while there, Eddy went skiing for exercise. He also took advantage of classes being offered by UCLA extension and took political science. Eddy became friendly with a young lady sitting next to him. She offered to pick him up from the base the following week for the class. Eddy was having dinner when a couple of officers started yelling for everyone to start cleaning up, because *the General was on his way*. Eddy opened the front door and saw his classmate exiting the back door of the General's limousine. Eddy got into the limo and said "Do me a favor and don't pick me up again."

He did not know the General was her father. He was so embarrassed in front of the group of guys.

A few days later Eddy was studying in the library when in walked the General. He did not know Eddy was friends with his daughter and came up to Eddy and asked, "What are you doing here"?

Eddy replied, "Sir, I'm studying to complete my Political Science class and get certified,"

"What makes you think you deserve to be certified?" asked the General.

Eddy got immediately upset and blurted, "Sir, if you would not be my General, I would ask YOU, *what makes you think you deserve to be a General?*"

The General stared at Eddy, never saying another word, turned around and walked out.

Eddy was very concerned that he would end up in the brig for being insubordinate, but he never heard anything about it.

While in Sapporo going out to bars and dances with friends, Eddy got caught where he wasn't supposed to be and lost his stripes. The woman lived with her mother. The father had been killed in WWII and now just the mother, this young woman, and two brothers lived in the family home.

After attending a dinner on a Friday Eddy said to his hosts, "I have to call a cab to go back to the barracks. "Why don't you stay here?" the mother asked. "I'll make a place for you to sleep."

The mother made a sleeping area on the floor...for two. He dated this woman for quite a while. She introduced Eddy as HER HUSBAND after that first sleepover.

***

During WWII some GI, or many GIs from who knows where, drew a silly cartoon face with the words, "Kilroy Was Here." One guy claimed and was awarded responsibility, but it was widely accepted to be a not-very-practical joke, a prank that soldiers around the globe played on everyone including themselves.

Ode to Life!

Eddy was known to have enjoyed the way the ladies reacted to men in uniform during his travels with the military. To this day, Eddy jokingly refuses to take any DNA tests.

During the time of the Korean War the Chinese ran over the 1st Calvary. They captured some Europeans who weren't even citizens. They said that even though they are in the military they had no rights because they weren't Americans. In order to change this, Congress passed a law that anyone who served 90 days in the U.S. military forces with honorable service could apply for citizenship. Eddy did it right away and that's why in 1953 he got his citizenship papers.

In two weeks they arrived back to the States and Eddy was discharged in Ft. Knox KY. because he had been drafted in Breckenridge outside Louisville. The year was 1954 and Ed was 25.

***

Also at this tender age of twenty-five Eddy found himself, for the first time all alone in the world. He had no direct family, no girlfriend, nothing to tie him down in any way. So, Eddy went back to Cleveland and back to the job he had before his military service. Naturally, it wasn't hard for him to get his old job back. He began running the bakery department, working the afternoon shift from two in afternoon to ten at night.

Always saving money and making more than he really needed, he bought a nice car and started looking for someone to share his life with.

While in the military they'd tell Eddy what he had to do and he followed orders. He knew you can't question the military. In fact he liked the military and while he was there he felt he owed a special allegiance to the U.S.A. They gave Ed a new life. It was the same division which had liberated him where he was allowed to serve. Now, he felt like he was 100% American and was proud of it.

One important lesson he'd learned in military life is to try and make changes and decisions when you are on top, rather than out of desperation. Also, he liked to try new things and even to look for problems just so he could see how to solve them. The time for change was now.

Ode to Life!

as told to Gordon Richiusa

Chapter Nine
Business & Pleasure

Eddy and Eveline got married in Philadelphia in 1957 on the last day of June.

***

Eddy was still working at *Rosen and Kasse's Bakery* in Cleveland. He and Eveline had been married about two years. Eveline was working at Wolf Brothers assisting the president of the company, quitting after only six months to avoid developing ulcers; bad, bad boss. After that, she got a job for Celanese Corporation running the front office. Now that was a great job in Eveline's eyes.

One day Eddy got a call from an Italian woman that he had previously dated. She and her husband owned a bakery. She told Eddy that she and her husband had a fight and she wanted to get rid of the bakery they owned together. Eddy hadn't heard from her for years, but she said she knew that Eddy was still baking and that she had an offer for him.

Apparently, her husband had come back from a delivery unexpectedly and found his wife making out with the baker in the back storeroom.

When caught, her lover ran out of the front and she ran out the back and left everything just as it was before she called Eddy that same night, "Eddy, I have to talk to you."

He said, "About what?"

"I want to sell you the bakery."

"I'll go have a look at it."

"Give me $1000 and it's yours, stock, lock and barrel."

Eddy was not interested in buying a store at the time and Eveline had a good job, but the price piqued his interest. He checked out the operation and then brought Eveline over for her final approval.

It had beautiful equipment: A ten by ten foot, thirty-two pan oven, really big. She included all the complete store equipment, two bread slicers, refrigerators, new doughnut frier, two big Hobart commercial mixers, and then they had the basement aluminum pans maybe four or five hundred Eddy estimated, and all the necessary raw materials, flour, yeast, etc.

Eddy knew that just the bakery without inventory was worth the asking price. He picked it up for $1000 which included everything in the inventory, including all the equipment.

So he quit his job as did Eveline so they could open their own bakery. He put a new sign up, "Hoffman's Bakery."

It wasn't easy because baking is hard work and Eveline had a difficult time adjusting, getting up every day at 3:00 am was not easygoing for her. She took over the front, managing the store. Eddy did all the baking in the back, with a little help from Eveline, except the Rye bread which needed a different type of oven.

He made French and Italian breads; he made small cakes, birthday cakes and cookies, Danish, donuts, pies, everything. The only problem was there wasn't enough foot traffic, and there weren't enough customers. People heard about the bakery and came from all over, but it wasn't enough. One day his father in law Simon said to him, "Why don't you sell everything and move to Philadelphia? It's better there."

The suggestion appealed to both Eddy and Eveline. They only had this shop for a year and didn't mind working, but Eddy was always trying to improve his and Eveline's situation. When they had the store, there were other drug store counters that sold coffee and cake, and Eddy went by a few of these, and said, "I'll bring over some merchandise. If you don't sell it I'll take it back, so you won't lose anything."

Eddy had started delivering to drug stores in the morning and things started getting better, but it was still too hard to make a living, so they liquidated the business. Eddy and Eveline put everything up for sale. Eddy couldn't sell the business itself because there were no customers for it, so he sold it piece by piece, and got about $15,000 that way. But he had bought it for only $1000.

***

They went to Philadelphia and Eddy got a job in the construction line, building new homes as a rough carpenter working for Eveline's uncle Harry who was in the building business. At first he framed basements, built shelves for the concrete, etc. When they came and poured the concrete they needed a way to keep it where the builder wanted it. Once it dried he went to the next one and once it dried Eddy would take the sides off and put the joints across.

He didn't care that he was doing construction. It didn't make much difference, as long as he was making money. He put groove floors down. Besides, he really enjoyed the work.

The builder saw Eddy could do a good job, and he made him his main helper, main rough carpenter, putting floors down, joists down, making sure everything was level and strong.

The problem was that in Philadelphia Eddy made good money when he worked, but it would rain so much during the week he couldn't work everyday. If it did rain no one could work in the construction industry, so when it did (which was a lot in Philly) Eddy took a train from Philly to NY and saw his friends. He also saw the money that they were making, around $250 per week, and at that time it was a lot of money.

It did not take long for him to ask himself, "Why do I have to do construction?" Eddy decided to go to New York and learn the fur trade.

He started off cleaning the floors for Cobrin Brothers at $55 per week. He saw his friend at another shop who did the nailing of furs. Eddy said, "Al, I will come after work and work with you for free. Won't cost you a penny. I want to learn what you do."

Finally, after 5 months he started receiving $95 a week at Cobrin Brothers nailing mink pieces, so he decided to talk to Al. "Al, you're making so much more money than me. I worked with you 5 months and I can do the work now." So, Eddy went to another furrier and said, "Look I just came from Europe. "I was a furrier there nailing minks and all that stuff."

They said, "Yeah, how much money do you want?"

"I don't want to be unfair, I will come in on a Saturday, and work for you all day. At the end of the day, you name how much you want to pay me. You tell me what I am worth to you."

Eddy had done quite a bit of work for the new boss who said. "You know, I can tell you are a European Furrier. I will start you out with $125 per week."

Eddy figured he got $95 at his old job so he went to Cobrin Brothers and said to the boss, "Look, what if you give me $15 a week more, Ill stay with you otherwise I have to leave."

"WHAT? WHAT! You started at $50-$55 a week and all of a sudden you want over 10% raise; *I have principles*!"

Eddy paused only a moment, "Alright, I'll give you a week's notice."

He went to the new job as a furrier. The guy Eddy worked for was more than pleased and Eddy got better and better because he was doing the work all day long, every week, and the new boss gave him more and more work and therefore more money By the time the season was in full force Eddy was making $250 per week.

He also did a lot of night work, when his usual shift ended. After four in the afternoon He went at night to another small company and he did the same work, making another $100.

In a few weeks Eddy's old boss, Jack Cobrin came around to see him. He said, "Eddy, you want to come back to work for me?"

It was the middle of the season, Eddy said "Why?"

He repeated himself as if he had practiced a script and Eddy simply didn't know the lines. "You want to come back to work?"

Eddy changed tactics, "You cannot afford me anymore."

He demanded, "Show me how much you are making."

"You see this?" Eddy showed him his paycheck for $250.

"O.K. I'll match it!" The X-boss said.

Eddy said, "Jack, you know if I leave my new boss in middle of the season he cannot get another guy...*I have Principles!* I mean really, I wouldn't do that to him."

Jack ignored the irony and said "I'll give you the same money you are making with him!"

Eddy said, "Jack. No." Jack's shoulder's slouched over and he walked away like a dog who had just been hit on the nose with a rolled up newspaper.

Eddy stayed with his new boss, and about 6-7 months later, he was making about $22,000 a year.

as told to Gordon Richiusa

By 1960 Eddy was making at least $500 a week, mostly in cash. So Eddy's instincts about becoming a furrier proved sound. The Union, assigned him to be Shop Chairman in charge of all the guys in the shop. If the boss wanted Eddy's crew to work overtime, he had to ask Eddy's permission.

Eddy didn't like that. Even if it was an hour or two and if Eddy said yes, he had to call into the Union and tell them he was working overtime. It was a lot of work and responsibility that was also paying off when the slow season started. However, Eddy somehow felt bad because it was not *his* business.

Sure, the boss had to ask Eddy's permission, but it didn't make sense to Eddy. That's the union way. Then Eddy was elected as an executive board member of the AFL/CIO, in New York. That's when he started to suspect that crooks always find a way to stick it to the little guy. It's been widely suspected that the mafia controlled these unions in New York.

Sometimes a union "steward" would come to the shops and tell the workers to slow down, or speed up or to stop work altogether based upon some agreement that had been made somewhere else.

The more Eddy saw corruption, the more he said to himself, "I have to quit." However, quitting a successful position at this level, making big money was not easy. At that time when minimum wage was around $80 per week

Ode to Life!

Eddy was making $250 officially. Besides it was not easy to quit the union.

***

So anyway one of Eddy's cousin Buni Gross had a seat on the NY stock exchange. You can't just go have a seat there. You have to pay for it. At the time it cost at least a million dollars for the "honor", and the seat holder had to show a bank account with another couple million to prove how much money they had and that they belonged in the group.

Buni and a top army engineer both retired from the army and went into business together, making specialty equipment for the atomic submarines. Buni inherited the entire business when his partner was killed in an accident. His company name was Electronic Enterprises and was on the Stock Exchange.

***

As Buni became more entrenched in the world of high finance, Eddy would get phone calls from him advising him toward certain investments. About 3 times he called Eddy and about 3 times Eddy lost money, and started to suspect that his cousin didn't really have the stock knowledge he was claiming to have.

Then the 4th time he called Eddy and said, "Eddy put as much money as you can on this one."

Eddy said, "Buni please, 3 times you gave me advice, and you were wrong. I lost money each time. Now this? I won't make the same mistake four times!"

Buni simply said, "BUY IT!" but Eddy wouldn't.

So, naturally that stock was called Xerox; It was selling for $28 per share. Eventually they split about 20 times, maybe more.

***

When Eveline was working on Fifth Avenue in New York for a Belgium company called *Eternit* translating French, she use to meet her dad when he came for shopping trips to buy merchandise for Milady Shoppe in Philadelphia. Eddy used to go with him sometimes.

This time with Eveline's father meant so much to her. They would go out to lunch together. Never while she was growing up did he treat her with such respect as now. It was very special.

In 1960 when Eveline got pregnant the Hoffmans were living in NY and she said, "I don't want to bring up children in NY. It's too crowded, and I don't feel safe here."

Eveline wanted to move to California, partly because her sister Jackie lived in the Bay Area and partly because she liked the city and the weather of San Francisco very much. Also she had stayed there for a short time away from Eddy before they had gotten married. San Francisco reminded Eveline of a cosmopolitan Paris.

When Eveline had her mind set on something, well Eddy had seen the power of his bride's resolve when she had told her parents she was marrying Eddy.

"Yes dear," was all that Eddy had said.

Ode to Life!

So, now it was only a matter of logistics. After the decision was made, it was only a short time before they packed up everything they wanted to keep and moved to California. This is how baby Joseph Hoffman had come to be born in San Francisco.

Joey Hoffman—was born April 9, 1961 in a hospital on a hill in the heart of San Francisco. The pregnancy was normal, but the birth was difficult. This was Eveline's first child and there was something else. Eveline was awakened between contractions and yelled at Eddy "stop shaking the bed, I need to sleep". Eddy was asleep nearby and said "I didn't touch anything". Then they felt the entire room shaking. "It feels like the whole hospital is shaking," Eveline said between contractions.

"That's because it IS," Eddy said matter-a-factly. They were having an earthquake. Actually, a magnitude 6.9 earthquake had struck off the east coast of Taiwan on April 9 at a depth of 35.0 km and the aftershock was just at this moment being felt in the hospital room. Eddy's experience with quakes was limited to his tour in Japan with the related tsunami. Eveline however, didn't have any experience, but California's and in particular San Francisco's reputation was well known.

To Eddy and Eveline, perhaps this was just another omen and unless the walls or ceiling started falling, they had more immediate concerns. All of a sudden things became complicated. It was decided that there had to be a bris. So, a rabbi was called from a local Temple to the hospital, and the surgeon performed the circumcision with a small ceremony. The Rabbi was not allowed to perform the ceremony at the hospital, so the surgeon had to do the surgery. Eveline was not happy with the way it was done.

Joey was tied down and was wrapped up like a semi mummy except for his head and groin area. Joey was screaming the entire time and Eddy had to hold Eveline down she was so upset.

Soon after returning home they made a discovery. Eveline found that Joey was allergic to her milk. He was projectile vomiting and very cranky from day one. So he was only nursed for three months. It was suggested they put the newborn Joey on fresh goat's milk after trying out different formulas, which really worked well, but was very expensive. Goat's milk is now well-known to be healthier for human-sized animals, than cow's milk because goats -- adults and babies--are more the same size animals as humans, as compared to a cow. Specifically, cow's milk is fortified with hormone's to make baby cows grow really big very fast. Giving cow's milk to human babies often results in digestive problems.

***

In 1961 there were only two places to be in the fur business in the United States. These were Los Angeles and New York. Eddy already knew he could make a great living as a furrier in New York, but now they were in California and decisions had to be made. Eddy decided to try to make a living in San Francisco. It was one of the few times he was simply unsuccessful.

He literally commuted back and forth to L.A. for a while, looking for work. He rented a place to live and drove back to San Francisco on the weekends. Los Angeles was the second largest fur market in the U.S..

Eddy did piecework on Rodeo Drive in Beverly Hills, and also for Rabin Furs in West Los Angeles.

***

Eddy got other jobs in a few other places downtown. It was apparent to employers that Eddy's work was superior, dedication allowed him to become skilled with very delicate work, which showed in his results. He was gaining a reputation especially for his chinchilla work.

Like every good husband, Eddy was very skilled at justifying pretty much anything for the sake of his family. He said to himself, "What's the difference in what I'm doing as long as I'm making a living?"

He had always had to hustle. In New York, hustling was the only way to make it. He knew that one must take opportunity where it arose. You can't just stick to one thing. If you see something better you do it, and no one could accuse him of every being lazy.

How could they? No matter what opportunity came Eddy's way, he grabbed hold with both hands.

***

For Eveline, as with most mothers, the years are marked and measured by the births of her children. About one year after Joey was born and the Berlin Wall was built (1961) Eddy and Eveline bought a cocktail bar. She recalled the Berlin Wall and the date of the cocktail bar purchase because of Joey's birth.

In the summer of 1961 Eveline moved to the L.A. apartment with Joey. Eddy was still making a good living as a furrier when Eveline got pregnant with Suzanne.

***

Suzanne was born December 14, 1962. Eddy was working in New York and commuting.

***

In 1961 is when Eveline's mother called and told Eveline that her Father had a heart attack.

Eveline's father had a heart attack in Philly and was in the hospital.

Eveline took Joey to the hospital and met her sister, Jackie there. "Jackie was not happy that Eveline wanted to take Joey in to see his grandfather, and Jackie argued with her. Eveline stood up to her sister, and took Joey in to see his grandfather regardless, which made Simon so happy. He had a huge oxygen tent over him and Eveline brought Joey into the tent and Simon gripped Joey's little hand.

Eveline did not want to excite her dad, so she didn't tell her father that she was pregnant with Suzanne. Four or five days later, he passed away at the age of 62. Seeing his grandson gave him the will to live just a bit longer. Eveline knew that her father wanted to retire more than anything else. For all his faults, Eveline felt that he deserved a few years of happiness because of the many spoken and unspoken horrors that he'd experienced in his life. She felt that he deserved a few years of peace. Unfortunately he died before he was able to fully enjoy his retirement.

***

Eveline's mother was running the store called Milady Shop that she and her father owned together, but now she needed help. Eddy had not gone to the hospital because he was busy in New York being a furrier-nailer, creating patterns on boards. So, when Eveline went into labor, Eddy rushed over as fast as the train from New York to Philly could carry him.

When Eddy got to the hospital, he was hoping for a girl, because the Hoffmans seemed to have an overabundance of boys and he'd already had Joey. He found a nurse when he arrived and asked about his wife, and whether his baby was a girl.

The nurse told him that she believed it was a boy and that before he could go into the room, he had to take care of the insurance paperwork, which he did. As he approached the birth room, the nurse called after him to correct her mistake. "It's a girl" she cried. Eveline had put a pink bow on Suzanne's head because she was bald unlike Joey with a full head of hair.

Less than one year after Suzanne's birth, John F. Kennedy was assassinated (Nov. 22, 1963).

***

The Hoffmans were living on Curson Drive where they had purchased an eight unit apartment in Los Angeles with Eddy's cousin. They also lived in and managed the building.

***

Carla Hoffman was born August 10, 1965.

She was born at Valley Presbyterian in Van Nuys.. She was a very fast pregnancy, almost didn't make it on time. Cousin Toby (also an Auschwitz survivor) brought dead flowers due to 110 degree weather. Harry Weiss, a Hungarian was the Landlord of the two bedroom duplex in Beverly Hills where they now lived.

In 1969 they bought the house where David would be born.

David didn't want to be born. He liked it where he was. A difficult birth, but the most lovable of the four babies.

***

In Philadelphia, they reunited with Herman Gross and Simon Gross--two uncles on Eddy's mother's side. One of uncles owned a **wholesale** fish store and the other opened a five and dime in a primarily black neighborhood. This Simon Gross had two sons and a daughter. Both of the sons were captains in the U.S. Army, in charge of buying whatever was needed for the military.

Simon had one daughter. She married a Polish guy who had been in the camps.

Ed warned the Uncles about the bad neighborhood. There was no walking traffic and the traffic they had was rough.

"How can you give such a dangerous place to your daughter?"

"Why, because it's a black neighborhood?"

"No because this is a dangerous neighborhood."

Five months later, both the daughter and her husband were shot to death in a robbery in the Five and Ten Cent store.

***

Luckily, Eddy always had his eye open for new opportunities so when he re-acquainted with a friend called Art who had spent time in the military with him, Eddy took a long hard look. His friend said, "Hey Eddy why don't we go in together and buy a cocktail bar?"

Eddy said, "I don't know anything about the cocktail bar business."

"Oh you'll be good." The old friend, Art was a bartender for his father. "We'll do great together."

Eddy could always spot an opportunity when it was presented, even when it was not apparent to anyone else--or even himself sometimes--at first.

Eddy thought, "What's the difference in what I'm doing as long as I'm making a living? I have to hustle here. It's the only way to make it. I've never been able to stick just to one thing, because if I am doing one thing and see something better I have to do it. I can never be lazy."

as told to Gordon Richiusa

They bought The Dog House in Los Angeles. It was on 6th and Alvarado, a rough area. Eddy didn't want to buy this place, but his partner said this was a good place, working class people, and that would come in every night. Eddy figured it was okay, but he saw a better place called the Stake Out in downtown LA near the courthouse.

"Nope, Eddy I don't want to have nothing to do with that." Art said.

So Eddy. went in with him at the Dog House. "I'll buy the place, but we aren't going to change anything plus the Dog House has been a registered name for 22 years, a corporation name, and I don't want to change that."

Art said, "How come? Why? We need to check into that."

Eddy said, "Leave it to me."

Eddy was a little concerned, because he thought he'd heard, even before he bought this business that there were other Hot Dog franchises called The *Dog House*. Weren't there Hot Dog stands all over L.A. with that name? But, this Dog House, in particular had been there for 22 years. It had a cute neon dog billboard with a wagging tail up front. This was a typical cocktail establishment with a few booths and tables scattered around a long, curved, wooden bar that dominated the building. Behind the bar was a door that led to a tiny storage area. Between the bar counter and the front exit door was a little pin ball machine, juke box, and cigarette machine. There was a little hallway with one restroom and the door to the storage. At the end of the hall was the door that led outside to the parking lot,.

So, when the previous owner of The Dog House, a Greek lady who wanted to sell the quaint and successful business to Eddy and Art for a mere $18 thousand, he went back to his Army buddy and said, "Art, I think we may want to hold off on the bar/restaurant investment. It's might be too much for both of us right now, but I found us another opportunity that we can start operating right way. It's just a well known bar called, The Dog House. There's only this one little potential problem." He told his partner about the other Dog Houses, but Art agreed that this looked like a good opportunity to strike out on their own and have their own business. He wanted Eddy as a partner, naturally, since he'd seen how success seemed to follow Eddy where every he went. "Look, Art," Ed said reassuringly. "If we need to, we'll go and put a lawsuit on the other Dog Houses; they have no business calling themselves The Dog, Houses because we own a corporation name that has been around for a long time."

Art says, "Are you crazy? Everything has been running smoothly for a while. Can't we just leave well enough alone?"

Eddy said, "Art, I'll find an attorney and it won't cost you anything to find out about this."

So they purchased the bar, and the corporation name. Eddy's idea was to keep the corporation in tact just in case, and he went into the cocktail bar business.

Art had one other stipulation, "I just want to be the president, O.K.?"

Eddy became Vice President. He didn't care.

Additionally, Eddy decided that since he really didn't want the headache of serving prepared meals, he would add to the countertop large jars of pickled wieners, in case anyone asked why the place was called The Dog House to begin with.

Art actually made the first attempt to find an attorney, opting for a very close friend who was an attorney in an attempt to get some free legal advice. His friend the attorney listened to Art's version of the problem and said, "There is nothing you can do about it. Forget it. It's just a name and it's not worth the hassle." Art then reported back to Eddy.

Eddy thought about it some more and decided to at least do some more research. "You know what Art? I'm for hiring my own attorney. I know a very smart attorney. Let him help us decide if it's worth pursuing."

When Eddy told his attorney what had transpired, he suggested that filing might lead to a settlement that everyone would be happy with. He agreed to pursue the issue further on contingency. If there was a settlement, he would take 1/3.

Ode to Life!

When Art heard about the new lawyer's suggestion he said, "I don't want any part of a lawsuit."

Eddy said, "Art, you know what, I will sign a piece of paper and give you $200 right now that allows me to look into this without you, but if I collect anything it's all mine. I mean come on, what's fair is fair right?"

Art said, "NO, NO, NO, NO." All of a sudden, he changed his mind.

Eddy said, "What do you mean no? If you want the $200 then sign the paper that you don't want anything to do with the lawsuit."

So they started down the road of filing a lawsuit and found out who owned the other Dog Houses which were franchised out individually. To their surprise, they were owned by IHOP, the International House of Pancakes!

The lawsuit was filed and almost immediately there was a response. IHOP wanted to make a deal with the bar owners.

"This is great, " Art said. "Whatever they offer, take it."

Eddy was cool though and with his lawyer's advice opposed jumping on a quick settlement. He told the lawyer to tell IHOP that the partners needed to talk and they didn't want to settle so fast.

There were many Dog Houses in the city and each individually could not settle. IHOP was going to have to settle for them all.

Eddy had them where he needed them. He and the other attorney sat down with IHOP's attorney to look over the offer from IHOP.

They offered Eddy and his partner $25,000 for the name only, 1/3 for the attorney. At first Eddy said *no*, thinking they could probably get a lot more.

Art said, "Take the money! Take the Money!"

Finally, Eddy agreed, "All right, let's settle."

So Eddy and Art got their $18,000 original investment back, which was what they had paid for the Dog House. They got to keep the place *as* the Dog House, but the *corporation* name needed to be changed, the original given over to IHOP. The Pancake conglomerate agreed to pay for everything.

The lawyer asked, "What do you want the new corporation to be called?"

Eddy responded, having already figured out the terms in his head, "I want it to be called the Puppy House."

So, the Dog House, became the Puppy House *on paper only;* they opened up the new corporation name and IHOP paid for everything and they got to keep the neon sign with the dog's wagging tail on the roof, as Eddy had requested.

They owned this cocktail bar with the neon dog for almost three years.

Since it was near a rehab and a questionable area, Eveline called it refined Skid Row. One of the customers who was Hungarian, would converse with Eddy in his native language. There was never any mention of the fact that the Hungarian Army had handed Eddy and his family over to the Germans on the fateful train ride to Auschwitz.

After a short time, The Dog House seemed to become the Hungarian hangout. More and more Hungarians, learning that the owner could speak the language came to the bar. They were a rough bunch, but they were loyal to their own...and Eddy was one of them, by decree.

"Don't worry, Eddy," they would say. We'll take care of you here," though they were just as quick to start a fight as end one.

***

One day, two Hungarian regulars were playing pinball in the back of the bar. One guy says to the other in a normal voice, "I'm willing to wager a whole $1 that I can beat your score!"

"You're on," said the other laughing, with no apparent attention being paid to either one of them by anyone else in the Doghouse.

Immediately a plain clothed police officer served a Notice of Violation to Eddy for allowing gambling. He did not even know that a wager had been made.

In a few days Eddy received a letter from the ABC Board (Alcohol Beverage Control) telling when he had to go to court to either defend himself or pay the fine.

You always knew when a cop came in. Eveline said she could smell them. Eddy said that you could tell because they always wore the same wrinkled suits and shined shoes.

One of the court reporters who was a customer at the Doghouse said, "You want a good attorney?"

"Sure, who do you suggest?"

That's how Ed met and worked with Charles Lloyd.

Charles Lloyd had been a police officer with Tom Bradley before he went into Law with his old partner, both African Americans. Tom Bradley had already made inroads into a political career in Los Angeles and would later become one of the most popular mayors in the City ever, having the International terminal at LAX named after him.

So, Charles was known to the courts as Bradley's partner when he went to court with Eddy, stood with him and made his opening remarks:

"Your honor, my client had no knowledge of any gambling, as he is being charged. It was merely a Gentleman's Bet on pinball machine that he had no knowledge of," Charles said.

"Dismissed," breathed the judge.

As the two walked out of the courtroom, Charles said to Eddy, "I won this case for you, but do me a favor next time will you kill somebody? I had to work too hard for you on this gambling case."

Tom Bradly later came to visit The Puppy House (that everyone still called The Dog House) and thanked Eddy, "...for trusting two Black Lawyers with your business." Both Bradley and Lloyd became regular customers when Ed and Eveline opened The Redwood House.

Ode to Life!

Eveline recalled decades later that The Mayor would always order, "A Beef Dip with mashed potatoes and extra gravy. He never touched alcohol."

***

The Dog House was in a very dangerous neighborhood. Fights broke out routinely inside the bar often times started by the Hungarians who saw themselves as Eddy's protectors.

During the Watts Riots these same Hungarians repeated the same mantra to Eddy, "Don't worry. We will protect you." Eddy was not too happy about receiving this "protection". For some reason the Dog House went unmolested, while many other storefronts were vandalized.

***

Then, there was the Robbery. Two guys came in and moved quickly. One struck Eddy from behind with a pistol and he was nearly knocked out. The other took the cash from the register and they rushed out before anyone could do anything. When Eddy got home around 3 a.m. Eveline was awakened from a deep sleep, reached over to touch Eddy as she usually did and noticed the bandages around his head.

Without hesitation Eveline screamed "Sell that business; it's too dangerous!"

Another time Eveline had been locked into the storage room (for her own safety) in the back of the bar when visiting. Eddy had allowed a homeless guy to sleep behind the supplies as long as he didn't cause any problems, but had not told Eveline about it.

Eveline had just about enough.

Eddy's temper and associated strength was legendary. He could stand a lot, but when he lost it, it was lost. One day Eddy went blank when two guys were fighting and wouldn't stop. Hungarians weren't there because they came in the evening.

Eddy found a baton behind the bar and was about to strike down the fighters.

"No, Eddy NO!" Marty, the waitress grabbed his arm when he raised the baton over his head. His rage had imbued Eddy with his legendary strength and while Marty held his arm, she was lifted off the floor.

Marty had been a customer first. Very friendly with the Hungarians. She drank all day long (screwdrivers) but never showed any signs of drunkenness. She was very smart and loyal to Eddy. She later got a job with a law firm across the street from the Chez Edouard and brought in a lot of business and always hung out there.

The bar was open from 6 a.m. to 2 a.m. Eddy and Art split shifts with a schedule that changed weekly so that neither would have to take a shift that was deemed undesirable. Each wanted to be fair to the other partner.

***

Next door to the bar, was an old hotel which a couple of French Canadians owned, Charles and John Tracy. John Tracy became a good friend of Eddy's. John used to go over to the Dog House, a daily customer. One while there he said "Eddie, my brother owns the hotel on 6th and Figueroa, you know Figueroa, next to the Johnathan club? My brother said the people who rent the restaurant in Charles' New Carlton Hotel are going bankrupt. If you are interested, come down and take a look at it, and you can make a deal with my brother, but only YOU."

This was the first that Eddy knew that John had a brother, and John made it clear that this was a deal ONLY for Eddy.

Eddy and Eveline went down there to take a look. It was very embarrassing for Eveline. It was a Topless Bar, one of the first Topless Restaurant bars in L.A. called *The Shillelagh*.

Even though Eveline could not raise her eyes to look at the topless waitress, she formulated the thought that the place was very nice inside, very high class considering what was happening.

The bankruptcy court locked up the place soon after this visit.

Eddy said, "Ok John I like the place and the people are going bankrupt so lets make a deal."

Eddy went down to Charles Tracy's house in Beverly Hills and also started talks with his attorney.

The partners sat down and Eddy said, "Charles, I'm a friend of your brothers and I want the place," then asked "How much rent do you want?"

Charles said, "You know what Eddy I'll give it to you for the same price I've been charging, $750 per month."

At the time that was a lot of money, but Eddy and Eveline agreed that it would be a good investment, and it would get them out of the Dog House. He responded quickly, "Ok it's a deal."

The place was basically in receivership, So Eddy got right into details, "The place is fine, but I want a five year lease, with a ten year option. I'll give you first month's rent-check and the last month's. That will be two separate checks," Eddy negotiated.

"Three checks," was the response. So $750 times three came to $2250, and that's what was paid.

Eddy made out the check and wrote the lease conditions on the back of the check itself.

Charles said "Eddy, consider it yours. I just have to send this check to my accountant and my attorney. I'll have the lease ready for you in five to seven days".

"All right," they ended it. "I'll give you a call once the papers are ready and you can open it up."

Eddy gave Charles the check and waited.

Eddy and Eveline waited 2 months, maybe longer, but Charles did not call.

Eddy also noticed that Charles had not cashed the check. And, still no call. Finally Eddy called him, "Charles, what's going on? I mean after all it's been a long time." So Eddy and his attorney went over to Charles Tracy's house.

"I was going to call you, but in the meantime what happened is I cannot give you a lease," said Charles.

"Why?"

"I sold the building to Bank of America," Charles said. "It's all right. Here is your check back. I didn't cash it."

"Fine," Eddy walked out and spoke with his attorney who said, "We can put a lawsuit on him for damages, for the lease, because he accepted your offer and kept your check for a long period of time without telling you anything."

Eddy said to his attorney "You know, his brother is a good friend of mine. I'm not suing a friend."

So Eddy went home and started looking for another business. Around two or three weeks later, Charles called Eddy back and said. "Eddy, I have to talk to you, again."

Eddy went to his home again with his attorney, "Ok what?" he asked.

Charles got right into it, "Eddy, before I couldn't give you a lease for a good reason. The building is now scheduled to be torn down, but it's not going to happen for five or even ten years. So, if you still want a deal for the next five or ten years before I have to tear the building down, you can open it up."

Eddy said, "Ok, but now how much rent do you want?"

Charles said "How much do you want to pay?"

Eddy figured in his mind that $500-550 would be fair, but turned it back to Charles.

Charles said, "I'm going to tell you how much I want."

Eddy said, "All right," expecting the worst.

Charles smiled and said, "You give me $200 per month. Is that all right?"

Eddy was shocked but didn't let on when he responded simply, "Ok it's a deal."

"Okay you start fixing it up," said Charles. "Hire the people you want and open it up."

Eddy asked if he could also have a room in the hotel as an office and was willing to pay an additional $50.

"In fact, I can give you office space on the floor above too at no extra charge."

So, that's what Eddy and Eveline did. Upstairs Downstairs, they took over the whole place!

Then, when things were settled with the topless bar, they turned the **Shillelagh** into **Chez Eduard *(Chayz Edwar--French accent pronunciation)***, an upscale businessman's restaurant cocktail bar, with little red candle lamps on every table.

This was a pretty sweet deal that just got better, because after a few months, Eveline realized that they were not being charged for any utilities. All the electric, water and gas was combined with the hotel.

***

1968 was a horrible year in U.S. history. Martin Luther King Jr. was shot April 4, 1968.

Then, Robert Kennedy was assassinated June 6, 1968.

Then, Bobby Kennedy was killed one block away, around the corner from the Chez. A customer came in and announced that, "Kennedy was shot!" All the high executives were there in the restaurant and everyone was shocked and saddened.

The clientele included all the big guys from IBM, Union Bank, Latham & Watkins (attorneys) and the like. It was a classy place. It wasn't a schlock place, but in the restaurant business--and Eddy's mind--there can be no rest. He was always looking for new opportunities.

***

Eddy had noticed a neighboring business, across the lobby of the same hotel. He called up Charles and said, "I see that the trophy store went out of business. What do you want for that store?"

Eddy didn't want someone else coming in with another food operation. Charles said "Uhhh, give me $100 per month." Eddy paid quickly and secured the store across the lobby side of the building and put in a deli with a beer/wine license. He prepared everything on one side of the kitchen and had a special deli man, George to take care of things. Eddy got so busy he had to hire three men to do nothing but deliver to the towers and attorney firms, who often ordered platters of food and pastries. George wanted to always be paid in advance so that he could go to Las Vegas. Eveline and Eddy did not accommodate.

***

In 1970, while operating the *Chez Eduard*, Eddy was invited to a Thanksgiving Dinner by a Native American. Eddy had several experiences in the military with Native

Americans, who he felt were the best. They were excellent soldiers and Eddy would rather have one of them fighting along side of him than anyone else. They are great fighters and very loyal.

Several Native Americans had lunch in Eddy's and Eveline's place. They were not afraid of heights, so they were putting up the steel frames (girders?) up on the 42nd floors across the street. One of the guys invited Eddy to Thanksgiving dinner on his reservation. Eddy didn't know his name or where the reservation was. This guy liked him for some reason and wanted to give him a horse. Eddy told him thanks, but "I'm too busy for a horse and too busy to take off work, and leave my wife to go to your reservation." Eddy was thinking to himself, "What the hell do I need a horse for?"

He couldn't understand why he was having a Thanksgiving dinner to begin with and asked, "Why? We took your land away, didn't we?"

"We invented Thanksgiving," the guy said, but Eddy still declined.

They stayed there six years before they tore the building down, but the deli was very successful; the workers who worked across the street constructing the building needed a place to eat. They stood outside about in a line half a block long everyday for lunch.

One day Eddy got a call about the Redwood House from a waitress who use to work there and also worked for Eddy. A restaurant that was kitty corner from the Times down on 2nd street, "Eddie this place is going out of business; it's called The Redwood House. Come and have a look." This was around the time Eddy received a notice that the hotel was being torn down.

The Redwood House was a beautiful place. Eddy put in a bid for $52,000, which included the stainless steel kitchen, walk in refrigerator, all inventory in a very classy environment. All the newspaper reporters from the Times would come into that place. Tom Bradley, the Mayor of LA was a regular customer, as well as a lot of judges, attorneys, etc.

Another person put in a bid for $75,000, but the judge knew Eddy and how he operated and gave it to him for $52,000. The downpayment was $30,000 for the place with a $22,000 note.

A union rep came by and asked, "Eddy, will you sign this contract?" And having had experience with unions, he said, "Wait a minute. It's not a done deal yet, don't rush it. You know why the people before me went bankrupt? It's because they had to hire extra people. They were very busy at lunchtime, but in the afternoon nothing. So, I want in the contract that I can hire part-timers, one or two part-time employees during lunchtime."

Eddy thought that was fair. The Union rep obviously did not agree. He said, "You sign this paper or we'll run you out of town."

Eddy said, "Get the hell out of here!"

So Eddy kicked them out and they put a picket line with many picketers right in front of the restaurant. The picketing went on for a long time but, in the meantime, Eddy knew what he was doing.

Because of the picketing Eddy lost about 40% of his business, but was able to cover expenses.

The bartender who had worked at The Redwood House for a long time had a friend who was an attorney, and they came in and said, "Eddy we want to buy you out. We'll pay what you paid."

"No thank you."

Every few months they came back and offered a better price. Ten months later they came and said, "Look Eddy, we'll give you $100,000 plus taking over the $22,000 note and pay for inventory." They wanted to get into the restaurant and cocktail bar business.

Eddy said, "I'll let you know, I'll talk to Eveline."

Eddy knew that he had a picket line for 8 - 9 months and would never give in. So, finally he agreed and said to each while pointing a gentle finger, "*You* are an attorney and *you* are a bar man. But, you are not a restaurant man and *he* is not a restaurant man. He is a bartender. He thinks bartending and running a bar are the same thing, but they are not. I want no notes, cash on the line." Eddy was trying to be as honest as he could, but was expecting that these partners would fail.

They said without hesitation, "It's a deal!"

Ode to Life!

By the time they paid Eddy off, he had gotten $115,000 total for the business and had only put down $30,000 for everything.

Eddy had the place for a year when he sold it to these guys with the warning, "You guys will go bankrupt."

They did.

"You know what Eddy?" they asked. "Why don't you stay with us for an extra month or two, and we will pay you to teach us how to buy, sell, and everything?"

Eddy agreed but the guys couldn't make a go of it, even with his help. It was 1973 and Eddy was 47 years old.

***

It took time. The bartender's brother, who Eddy had no idea was a big union official in Philadelphia was channeling money into the restaurant. Less than three years later, they had to close up. Perhaps, that brother got into trouble.

The landlord called Eddy and said, "You know what Eddy? When we gave you the lease it was for ten years, and you are still on the lease. Will you come back and take over the restaurant?"

Eddy didn't want to start again with the union.

He had been fairly successful and even with the strike made a living and had no other problems. Even so, about 40 percent of Ed's business was gone because a lot of judges and attorneys didn't want to take sides against the Union. Eddy understood that. He had a big clientele from the LA Times including many reporters every night. Most of them didn't want to see the place close either.

Some of the attorneys and the secondary customers donated a whole weekend to go to court to get an injunction and force the Union to allow Eddy to operate with only two part-time picketers, so as not to violate the purpose of the picket but allow the lunch rush to be relatively unmolested. It worked. The injunction was put into place. What did it cost for all the high paid lawyers? Eddy and Eveline served them a steak dinner.

Eddy, as usual had already thought everything through. He knew that the landlord had no legal standing. When the business was sold, the lease with Eddy became invalid.

***

One of the suppliers for the Redwood House was Jungee Nakamora. He represented Santory Company, primarily known for their whiskey. A large group of executives from Japan, about eighteen or twenty in number, were brought in to see where Jungee was selling their liquor.

They took up a whole room and Ed personally wanted to impress his guests, so he brought a round of Sapporo beer to the table, reasoning that it would be seen as a gesture of respect because Sapporo was a Japanese product.

"What? Sapporo? We will never drink a competitors beer!" One of them shouted.

Ed had not realized that this simple gesture might topple an otherwise positive relationship. Instantly he responded, however, "How will you ever know if your beer is better if you never taste the competitor?"

Suddenly, the stern faces of his former enemies of WWII all broke into laughter. Everyone at the table applauded Ed's response and the atmosphere lightened considerably. So much so, in fact that they made an interesting offer to Ed, "We're opening a bar in Tokyo. We want you to come and run the place for us!"

The best Ed could think to say at that point was, "I'll think about it." Later he went home and told Eveline what had transpired.

"Move to Tokyo? Are you nuts?"

That was the end of the conversation.

***

Shortly after this, Eveline's mother liquidated the Milady Shoppe, and she moved to Los Angeles to be near her daughter. Eveline found her an apartment a couple of blocks away. At that time Anna, Eveline's mother, gave her daughter mementoes from their past. Among them was the yellow Jewish Star that Anna was forced to make and wear during the German occupation. It has come to mean a lot to Eveline over the years.

After some years went by Eveline shared the Star with her younger sister Paulette who had the star framed. When Jacqueline decided to write her book, *Chased By Demons*, she asked Eveline to loan it to her for reference.

After many years the star found its way back to Eveline and is placed among other valuables in her dining room hutch.

***

Eveline and Eddy then decided to go into the *implant* cafeteria business. That's when a big factory or some other corporate building, lets someone run a cafeteria *within* their facility. Eddy and Eveline had two cafeterias, with two different companies that had between them 800 to 1300 employees at one time. The business was inside two large, separate factories, one in Los Angeles, the other in Torrance. One good benefit of such an arrangement is that Ed and Eveline usually had weekends off as well as holidays.

The first one Ed bought was called *ProtoTool* Company. They gave him a monthly check, a subsidy to try and keep prices down and give good service. The subsidy was $750 per month. They also didn't charge Ed rent, electric or telephone, no gas bill no nothing. If anything broke down the company fixed it. Ed also had around ten or twelve vending machines and they worked nicely also. The store closed at 4 p.m. They had about 800 people working at ProtoTool. Meanwhile another place opened up in Torrance, and a business agent contacted Eddy saying, "Eddy, you'll want to buy it; it's a very good deal."

So they bought a second (implant) at *Tridair* Corp. Tridair shared the building with *Brownline*, combined together with about 1,200 people working there.

Originally, a food-truck operator had been bringing his mobile eatery into the parking lot. Then, they asked him to bring his business *into* the building, which he did. That's who Eddy and Eveline bought the second cafeteria from, with a payment known as *goodwill*. This means that the asking price was based on the money that was being received as gross profits.

Eddy purchased this second business with, as usual, special amendments. The CEO of Tridair said, "Eddy we want you to make a profit. Our company is going to buy a cup of coffee for everyone of our employees in the morning. We will send you a check monthly to cover the cost. It amounted to about 10 cents a cup, per every cup for every employee regardless if the coffee was consumed or not.

The coffee Eddy provided cost the company a little less than regular price, because not everybody drank coffee in the company for one thing. Not only that but if anybody came in and also didn't drink coffee, the company gave them discounts on other drinks like soda or milk. Eddy and Eveline also catered the company parties, retirements, holidays, birthdays etc. So every month Eddy was getting about $3000 profit from just this second company, and he didn't have to pay any rent or utilities! The company also sent janitors to clean the cafeteria.

The only expense he had was a fast order cook, two women and one Mexican guy, an older gentleman who made the coffee and did odd jobs like fill the vending machines all around the plant.

Ed ran the one site and Eveline ran the other. Then they moved from Beverly Hills to Rolling Hills Estates in Palos Verdes, because David had a problem breathing. The doctor was concerned that if The Hoffmans stayed in the Los Angeles area, David would develop asthma. Los Angeles had a bad smog situation in those days. On many days people were asked to curtail their activities until the smog alert was cancelled.

The doctor said to the Hoffmans, "As long as you live in Beverly Hills your son will have problems."

Pollution was out of control in much of the country, but Los Angeles air was extremely poor much of the year due to all the cars on the roads.

So, they went and sold the Beverly Hills house , which it turned out was a double blessing since the Tridair cafeteria was close to Rolling Hills Estates. It was on Lolita Boulevard, in Torrance. But Eddy always looking for a better situation decided to sell the Proto Tool business downtown.

***

After six years at this location, Eddy sold to a Korean husband and wife. The husband had been after Eddy, wanting to get in on the Gravy Train for a while, so Eddy finally gave in and said, "Alright."

Eddy told him how much he wanted. He also suggested to the new owner that the transition should be methodical.

Ode to Life!

He recommended for him to come in and work a whole week as cashier while Eddy stayed on with him. "You can see what we are doing. You'll see how much we take in and everything else."

"Oh yes yes yes," The prospective owner said.

Eddy did not trust that this effort was going to be a success and asked for cash in the transaction, which was paid.

Eddy could see that his suggestions were falling on deaf ears. "Don't let the cook go; don't change the girl in the back; don't do anything different because these are our factory workers, and make sure that you don't just hire your relatives!" he warned.

"You cannot have Asian food all the time. You need to let the customers get used to you." The Korean buyer acted like he loved all of Eddy's suggestions.

So after Eddy sold him the business, this is what happened. The Korean went into the place and against Eddy's suggestions he fired everybody. Then the new owner took his brother-in-law in as the cook and his wife became the cashier while some other girl, probably a family member was there to help out.

Almost immediately he was losing money. How can you lose money when you get a subsidy for $750 with no other expenses? He found a way.

The other problem as Eddy saw it was that the immigrant Koreans seemed to always want only relatives to work in their stores. The wife was there, without any experience but feeling as if she was in on the deal.

Once in a while Eddy would stop in and try to smooth out the transition, but each visit proved that things were not going smoothly at all. One day, one of the factory workers was being grilled by the wife-cashier. Eddy had put a candy counter in near the cash register when he was in charge. When you walked in there were things to occupy the customer.

This worker had a candy bar sticking out of his pocket, and the wife was practically yelling at him, "Are you sure you didn't put anything in your pocket!?"

It's never a good idea to insult your customers! If somebody eats a candy bar without paying, forget it. It's not worth a lousy fifty cents. Anyway, most everyone was honest enough to pay what they owed even without Eddy or Eveline having to tell them.

So, here was the new owner's wife accusing one of her customers of a theft that the customer was obviously not trying to cover up. The candy bar was probably his already, Eddy thought.

The Korean owner ended up suing Eddy, as if he'd misrepresented the value of the deal, but Eddy won the case. Eddy went to court and explained to the judge that he had even offered to have the husband work the cash register for a whole week to see what the business was like before buying it. The new owner's attorney, who was also Korean, was mad at Eddy's attorney, possibly because Eddy's attorney had all the evidence in Eddy's favor; Eddy had to have an attorney to protect himself; The owner's attorney wanted to take James Jess, Eddy's attorney, outside and fight him. He finally cooled off; Eddy thought the whole thing ridiculous.

Eddy's attorney knew him well and knew his client wouldn't cheat anybody. Eddy ran an honest and profitable business. He believed in the pillars of honesty and being straight forward with everyone.

Whoever came into one of Eddy's establishments would always get their fair share and a little extra, always! That's the reason that Eddy and Eveline always did ok in business. The customers recognized this and were loyal.

When Eddy had the restaurants he never charged for hors d'oeuvres. He had two busboys, and all they did was serve hors d'oeuvres and clean the tables: Pigs in the Blanket, Miniature Cheese Burgers, homemade potato chips, little things like that. These were served on plates and most people decided that they wanted drinks with their hors d'oeuvres. That was a good bargain in Eddy and Eveline's opinion.

***

These successes were not without problems. Suddenly, in one instance the Bakers went on strike. This was not a real problem as Eddy baked his own bread and rolls. He used to do a lot of hands on running the full cafeteria. He would go into the cafeteria on the weekend and prepare enough cherry, apple and peach turnovers as well as cinnamon rolls, etc. for the entire week.

Before these were in the oven people would come up and say, "*Save me two of those apple ones,*" or "*Put aside for me four or five peach.*"

The turnovers were all puff pastry, very light and flakey. Eddy would do the bite test which was, if you bite into a pastry and it disappeared in your mouth then it was good enough to sell.

He used to sell a lot! As a matter of fact some other companies would send a person over to buy a couple dozen pastries. Even outside of the factory they asked permission to come in and look at Eddy's operation...just look and also buy some pastries. They always wanted to learn more. Eddy had the knowledge of baking and other things that many people did not because they were trained in America. He was a European baker.

Being a good baker depends on understanding many important details: how you mix, how you bake, how hot the oven is supposed to be, what ingredients and their portions. Everything has a recipe which must be followed to get the expected result.

Eddy knew that when you start making something it might end up being completely different from what was expected. If mistakes happened, you did not try to force the issue. He would put the oven up to over 410 degrees on one item and down to 350 degrees for another.

Ode to Life!

A lot of people came into the cafeteria just for coffee and pastry. Eddy sold a lot of pastries. They were his specialty. People came from all over just to get a turnover.

***

Ed had twelve vending machines in each cafeteria, for a total of twenty four. That was a headache to Eddy because every weekend he had to empty the money from the machines, and then take all the quarters, dimes and nickels and wrap and count stacks of coins by hand from each machine. It was a lot of work, but the profits mounted.

Also in the companies, Eddy carried credit for some of the employees for short times.

When someone came to work with one of the companies Eddy kept a list of everyone's name on one side. On the other was how much each person owed and if they spent $3 or $4 on any given day. Whatever each customer spent he put on the other side of the list so he always knew how much everyone owed. It was a lot of paper work for both of them.

The tallies always consisted of about 50 or 60 percent in charges. So at the end of the week, when people got paid they gave Eddy or Eveline their check and Eddy went to the bank and cashed them. He deducted what was owed him and gave back the rest minus one percent, which he had to charge, because the bank charged that as a transaction fee (even in those days).

In the afternoons Eddy would go down to the wholesale market and stock up on produce and whatever else was needed, just like the old days. He knew what was required to run a cafeteria.

For sodas he bought both Pepsi and Coca Cola, 300 to 500 cases at a time. He had to consider storage, because he bought so much from Coca Cola he felt he needed a refrigerator with a glass front.

Coke charged fifteen dollars a month in case the machines broke down. If that happened they promised they would fix it or bring a new one; this arrangement was only valid however as long as Eddy didn't use the Coca Cola refrigeration for Pepsi. Coca Cola hated their rival so much that they didn't want their products in the same storage area.

When Pepsi found out what Coca Cola was doing, the Pepsi Company gave Eddy a refrigerator also, and Eddy wasn't allowed to put Coke in there. The coffee maker was given free of charge from Farmer Brothers Coffee.

This was not the first time that Coke and Pepsi were at odds. When Eisenhower was president the Soviets and U.S. were just beginning to see everything in terms of opposing ideologies. At one point the American government arranged the *American National Exhibition* in Moscow and sent then-Vice President Richard Nixon to attend the opening.

The businessman's fable goes like this: American business interests were anxious to begin trading in the Soviet Union. Somehow Vice-President Nixon was left alone with Nikita Khrushchev to debate with the Soviet leader the finer points of capitalism vs. communism. Their conversation got ugly, fast (both men were notorious for losing their cools in debates) so at one point the vice president of Pepsi bartered a truce and offered the Soviet leader a cup of the beverage which had become Coca Cola's biggest competitor.

Naturally, since Coke was closely identified with Americanism (even though Pepsi was an American bred company, as well) Khrushchev decided that he loved Pepsi.

Years later, the people of the Soviet Union wanted to bring Pepsi products to their country permanently. However, there was an issue of how they would pay for their newest beverage, as their money wasn't accepted throughout the world.

So, the enterprising communist country decided to buy the Pepsi using a universal currency: vodka!

In the late 1980s, Russia's initial agreement to serve Pepsi in their country was about to expire, but this time, their vodka wasn't going to be enough to cover the cost.

So, the Russians did what any country would do in desperate times: They traded Pepsi a fleet of subs and boats for a whole lot of soda. The new agreement included seventeen submarines, a cruiser, a frigate, and a destroyer.

The combined fleet was traded for three billion dollars worth of Pepsi! Russia loves Pepsi.

The exchange allowed Pepsi to become the 6th most powerful military in the world for a brief time, before they sold the fleet to a Swedish company for scrap recycling.

***

He also had special deals going with local butcher shops, including the Kosher butcher shops.

Eddy went to some of them and said, "You guys grind a lot of hamburger meat. I would like to buy my meat directly from you. Could you put ground beef into packages of ten pounds each, and freeze them for me?"

When the butchers had 200-300 pounds he'd go by and pick up the packs. He knew that each butcher would have to get rid of that meat somehow and a 200 pound order was ideal. So, Eddy got his meat directly from the butchers for 50 cents a pound.

If he went through the suppliers it was $1.60-$1.80 per pound because they were paying their employees to do the packaging, pick up and delivery that Eddy was having done at the source or doing himself.

Whenever he needed meat for hamburgers or tacos he just took it out and defrosted between ten and thirty pounds. Because of all the special deals, he had freezers all over the place.

Other business were aware of the situation and people from these suppliers used to call him saying, "Eddie I have 300 or 400 pounds of ground beef!"

Eddy always paid them cash right away and took off their hands as much as he could store. Everybody won. The butcher could sell their entire inventory and Eddy knew that 1 pound of good ground meat could make three hamburgers. A big hamburger or cheeseburger could then be sold much lower than his competitors, so low in fact that Eddy was still making a really good profit.

***

One day Dave Gold saw a company he wanted that had gone bankrupt and was having a big restaurant sale of equipment. Eddy went with Dave to split the cost if they could make a good deal. Dave told Eddy about his idea for having a store where everything was just 99 cents. He asked Eddy if he wanted to be his partner when he started these 99 Cent Stores. He developed close to 100 stores and then his company got on the NYSE. The stock hovered around $20 to $21 per share in the beginning of which Dave owned 74 million shares or about 60%.

Eddy always thought of Dave as being very eccentric. He was a very nice guy and he would do anything for Eddy, but he just wasn't organized. He had everything up in his head.

In that regard he was very sharp, very quick. Once when Eddy and he were walking in downtown Los Angeles, there was an old guy in a random store, no customers around. Dave looked in through the doorway and walked up to the old man and said, "You know how about we make a deal, I'll buy everything you want to sell, stock, lot and barrel. What do you think of that?"

***

So the guy asked what he felt was a fair price. Dave looked around a minute and said,"Okay," and handed over a check adding, "Talk to the landlord," just like that he acquired one of his 99 cent stores.

It was a hardware store. The whole deal took him just a few minutes. Apparently Dave wanted to give Eddy's son Joe a job in this store, to learn how to run it and make a business career for himself.

***

But when Joe found out about it he said, "I'm not taking the bus all the way Downtown L.A. and back to work!"

"So, you're giving up a great deal," Eddy barked and walked out. He always felt as he did then, that his son would have been better off to take the offer. Joe now regrets that he didn't take the offer.

***

Dave Gold and his wife came to Eddy and Eveline's 45th wedding anniversary party. When Dave came in there were about 60-70 people. He took out a big bunch of 99¢ Coupon Books and handed them out to all the guests. Then he said, "Eddy, I want you to have a good time on me."

"Really?"

He then took an envelope from his pocket and gave it to Eddy who didn't even look at it until later. When he and Eveline opened the gifts later, they found that the check from Dave was in the amount of $999.99.

***

At his warehouse later, Dave said, "Eddy, sit down. I want to show you something."

Ode to Life!

Every Wednesday or Thursday Dave had all the sales people come into his office who sold Dave their merchandise. Sometimes they'd have a truckload of merchandise and he'd say to them, "Now sell it to me for the lowest price you can give me. If I agree, I will buy the entire lot. If I don't like your price, I will say *no*...period, and you might as well leave with your merchandise, no second offers." Even if you offer a better deal the second time.

"All right, so you gave me the best deal you could, right"? He was showing Eddy how he handled the sales people. If he or any of them said "no" he didn't buy anything. It didn't matter if they tried to lower the price of the goods to $.01 on a second bid. But, if they said "yes" he bought the whole thing, right then and there.

***

Another time when Eddy was at Dave's place he noticed that Dave sold lotto tickets, so he was selling them for 99¢ instead of a dollar so he was taken to court. He said "Look I put out the extra penny what's the difference?"

The court said 'NO!' and took out all the lottery tickets from his stores. Eddy had tried to warn Dave that the Lottery people would not go for this.

***

In 1990 Eddy retired from all his businesses. He was sixty-two years old. Now, he had too much time on his hands so he got a job with Honey Baked Ham. He was the production manager for manufacturing and was managing a store in Torrance for a couple of months.

Then, they switched him over to near the airport where they had another Honey Baked Ham store. This lasted for a little more than two years. He felt he had to do something.

In the meantime, Eveline was still working for Jenny Craig. She was one of the best consultants on the West Coast, very good at representing the company. Eddy believed that she was so savvy because she had spent most of her life with him, and Eddy said that he had programmed her that way. Eveline does not agree with this assessment!

***

In 1972 Eddy and Eveline decided that they wanted to go to Israel together.

Coming off the plane Eveline saw soldiers surrounding the plane and the airport. She smiled. She was having a completely different feeling about the rifles they had on their shoulders than the images she had in her head. She had always harbored a feeling or uneasiness around guns, especially rifles. Many seemed to be armed here, but somehow that feeling of uneasiness was gone. These soldiers, both men and women, she knew were there to protect her. Without any overt actions on anyone's part Eveline felt welcomed, safe, a feeling that she did not always have.

The armed soldiers were smiling and calm. People were approaching them with questions and they were happy to respond. When Eddy and Eveline passed through customs, they went to a nice hotel and there they were met by the friendly smile of Eddy's Aunt Linka.

Linka held a bouquet of flowers, which she handed to Eveline and followed this up with numerous hugs and kisses for her favorite nephew and his wife.

Aunt Linka--Eddy's father's sister--had lived in a nearby Falau to the Hoffman's when Eddy was growing up. That nearby town was technically in the city of Huszt.

Everyone of that era was immersed in the ancient traditions and culture of their family so it was not unusual that in 1925 Linka had been the bride in an arranged marriage to a suitor in another nearby falau. This she did without complaint, even though it meant that she would not be allowed to marry the first love of her life.

Her first marriage lasted until 1943 when both she and her husband were taken into Auschwitz. Her husband was killed there, but somehow Linka managed to survive.

When she was liberated she returned to her homeland. She had known that her sweetheart had also married another person, but what she only found out after her liberation was that her first love's spouse was also killed in Auschwitz.

After Liberation, these two returned as widow and widower to a land now called *Ukraine* which was under Russian military control.

Right away upon their return to their homelands, they were reunited, and very soon after they got married, each for the second time as their first spouse had been killed while in slavery at Auschwitz.

Linka's second husband passed away several years later, and that is when she moved to Israel. Eddy and Eveline visited her during this time, their first visit to Tel Aviv.

In a tragic twist of fate, after Eddy and Eveline had returned to the U.S. and during the period where Iraqi SCUD missiles were being launched regularly into Israel, one of these bombs hit her building and killed Linka and two other gentlemen who lived there.

Eveline and Eddy were watching the news here in their Rolling Hills Estate home when this happened, but did not know at the time that a woman shown on the television being carried out on a stretcher was Aunt Linka. They were informed about her death the next day.

***

In 1997 Eveline and Eddy Hoffman went to Europe so Eddy could revisit Scotland and Ireland. While there they visited James and Greta, relatives of their next door neighbor in Palos Verdes. Eveline remembers seeing many Long Haired red Cattle. She was quite taken with them, so beautiful. They met a man who was a tour guide in Milisle who had written an article about the Orphanage where Eddy had been. Bobby Hackworth was 11 years old when the Jewish children had first arrived at the farm in Millisle. Bobby had found an old photograph of the children who had lived at the orphanage. In the photo was Eddy Hoffman.

***

They bought the house in Rolling Hills Estates, Palos Verdes for $215,000 and stayed there from 1980 until moving to Laguna Woods Village in 2004; Laguna Woods Village is the old Leisure World community in southern Orange County. The Palos Verdes house sold for $1.1 million. That was a good return.

They felt they were lucky to sell that house because they decided that they weren't going to hire the regular real estate people. They signed an agreement with Help U Sell.

This was a company that had a set fee for everything anyone needed to sell a property, they said. One of the only catches a seller faced was that every morning you had to take out the *for sale* sign and put it on your lawn. At night you would bring it in again. That was the rule. They also had to do their own open houses.

If someone showed interest, the Help-U-Sell people came and took over the negotiations. All the seller was required to pay was $8,000. A standard real estate agent commission would have cost them 6 percent, $66,000 for the same sale.

***

Eveline and Eddy sat down with their four children,--all college aged or approaching it by now--Joe, Suzanne, Carla, and David, and they said, "Look, we're going to pay for all your tuitions, all of your books, everything. The only thing we're asking is that you try and get as good grades as possible, and we'll give you monthly pocket money to live on, also." The two boys chose not to take the deal.

All the children finished high school and both of the daughters took the offer and went to college. Susanne went to Humboldt State. Carla went to San Diego State University. They both finished. Carla graduated with a degree in economics and Suzanne became an English teacher.

Eddy talked to Suzanne and said, "In the beginning, as a teacher you will have so much problems with tenure and all that. Please don't bother! You are smart. Go to work during the summer time in private industry and see how you like it. Find something that will prevent you from having to rely on teaching as a career." Suzanne took her father's advice once again and got a job at Seiko in Torrance.

***

When Eddy and Eveline had gotten married Eddy said, "I would like to have four kids to replace my family who perished, and because my mother had four boys. My mother's side of the family had four girls. So four seems like a good number."

They ended up with four children and grandchildren as well, three boys and one girl.

When the Twin Towers were struck, the Hoffmans were babysitting in San Diego, Colin (a grandson, Carla's first born).

Ode to Life!

As Colin grew he had always shown a special interest in his grandparents' past and would ask non-stop questions of every detail. Sometimes Eveline thought that Eddy was taking advantage of their grandson's sincerity for the sake of a joke.

"Grandpa, what would you eat when you were a boy in Czechoslovakia?"

"We had breakfast, eggs, cereal, toast, the usual. The big meal was dinner...."

"Where was Meme born?"

"Paris (he pronounced it *Paree*), France."

"Oh really? What do they eat there?"

"Frogs legs and snails mostly."

"What do they manufacture?"

"Perfumes mostly."

"Perfumes? Why?"

"The French don't like to take showers."

***

One day, a friend named Sydney called.

Sydney had come to USA before Eddy did, but Eddy was drafted right away and was sent to Japan. When Eddy came back to the states he worked in the fur line and he was reunited with his old friend. Sydney and Eddy saw each other every day and then Eddy moved to California.

In 1958 Sydney started buying up some dilapidated buildings in New York, and he hired people to paint and refurbish them, then he rented them out. So when he called Eddy years later, he said, "Eddy, you me and your wife let's go to Europe."

Eddy said, "Sydney, right now I can't because I just sold my house for $1 million and I'll have to give the IRS about $42,000 to pay the taxes."

Sydney responded, "That's nothing Eddy. You know what? If you want to go, tell me how much you need and I'll send it to you. You don't have to pay me back."

Eddy said, "Sydney I appreciate it but no thank you. You know I don't want to take someone else's money".

Sydney countered, unfazed, "What do you think I paid in taxes last year?!"

Eddy said, "I have no idea $100,000?"

"Not even! That's a spit in the ocean. I paid $20 million in taxes last year."

Eddy was shocked until Sydney explained why? It seems that Sydney had sold *eighteen* buildings to a bank who paid him so he spent $20 million in taxes! His profit for the buildings was still $60 million!

Eddy and Eveline decided to go on the trip, but they paid for it themselves.

***

Eddy always thought of Sydney as kind of a weird but kindred spirit. When Sydney came to U.S. he didn't have money to buy cigarettes, Eddy remembered. Now about 6 years later, Eddy, Eveline, Sydney and his wife Sylvia went to Europe traveling all over the place.

By this time, Sydney was very well to do. Eddy found him to be a funny guy. Sydney was caught up in the economics of the past. During this trip, while staying in a nice hotel, Sydney came down to breakfast. He could afford the whole kitchen by now, but to Eddy's surprise he took a big napkin and put a lot of food down onto it, folding the corners like a hobo getting ready for a journey.

Eddy said," What are you doing Sydney?"

"I want to take it with me; I don't want to have to buy food during the day," Sydney replied without shame.

Eddy felt that he had earned the right to speak his mind and not hold back his words, "Sydney you're embarrassing me and that's not right."

"I'm used to doing this Eddy".

Sydney owned, at the time four large buildings in Long Island. One of the buildings had two big stores inside of it. He was getting $50,000 each a month for rent plus what he'd earned from the other eighteen buildings on top of that. They all enjoyed the rest of the trip.

***

When they were coming back home from Europe Eddy. realized that Sydney's wife was developing memory loss. Now, she is still alive but can't recognize anyone. Sydney still takes care of her and about eight months ago called and said "Eddy let's go to Europe again."

Eddy said, "Sydney I can't right now, how about next year? How about you come over here for a little bit."

Sydney said "No I cannot leave my wife, because she has 24 hour care but I'm tired being at home. I'll let you know if I'm coming."

So about three or four weeks later Eddy got a call that Sydney had a heart attack and passed away. He left $160 million to his two sons. When he got to the U.S. he couldn't even afford a pack of cigarettes and had been with Eddy in the German concentration camps.

At the end of his life, a man who has survived the same camps as Eddy, was a success. He may have worn a rug on his head, a terrible toupee that Eveline always noticed but was polite not to mention. He had come from the same area that Ed had grown up in and this vast fortune was quite a legacy.

Ode to Life!

as told to Gordon Richiusa

Chapter Ten
The Sweetest Fruit

When Eddy was a child growing up on the farm, not only did he learn that the sweetest fruit fell from the tree, but that somebody still had to pick up the fruit for everyone to enjoy. He knew that opportunities would present themselves, but they seldom presented themselves more than once.

***

So, when Eddy had gotten a job on Rodeo Drive and a few other places, he was really honing his skill of making the right decisions. The fur business was already having problems with animal activists, but Eddy had decided to make a reputation for himself as a capable furrier who could do very delicate chinchilla work. Opportunities continued to present themselves.

When the Alfred Hitchcock movie, The Birds was filming, the producer decided he needed two mink coats for the female lead, Tippi Hedren. This job went to Eddy. When you watch this movie and you see Tippi Hedren wearing furs, they were created by Eddy.

Soon after, however, it was reported in the news that a model had fake blood poured on her for wearing real furs. Eddy, always growing up in the world of animal husbandry did not think it immoral to be in that business. He had even made fur collars, capes, and hats for his little daughters.

***

There was a business neighbor next to The Dog House, an old hotel which a couple of French Canadian brothers owned, Charles Tracy and John Tracy.

With this close connection, John Tracy became a good friend of Ed's, and used to come over to the Dog House and have a drink now and then. One day he came to Ed and said, "Eddie, my brother owns the hotel on 5th and Figueroa, you know Figueroa? The Johnathan club?"

The hotel at 5th and Figueroa was an old hotel that was beautiful. John said to Ed, the people who own the restaurant downstairs of the hotel it are going bankrupt."

So, Ed and Eveline went down to take a look. To both of their surprise it was a Topless Bar, one of the first Topless Bars. Restaurant bar. Very nice inside, very high class. So whatEd says "Ok JohnEd like the place and the people are going bankrupt so I'll make a deal."

Ed drove to Charles Tracy's house in Beverly Hills and they started talking and with Ed's attorney. They sat down and Ed said "Charles, I'm a friend of your brothers. I want the place and said how much rent do you want."

He said, "You know what Ed, I'll give it to you for the same price $750 per month. At time that was a lot of money you know.

Ed spoke evenly, "Okay, it's a deal."

The place was basically a receivership. So, Ed said "Ok fine, the place is fine, but I want a 5 year lease, with a 10 year option. I'll give you first months check and the last months. Two months pay. Three checks."

Seven hundred and fifty times three equals two-thousand, four hundred and fifty. Ed made out the checks and wrote out the conditions on one of them, like a tiny contract. He said "Eddie", Ed's attorney was with me he said "you consider yourself it's yours, you just have to send this check to your accountant, for the attorney, and make out the check for the lease and its yours. ."

"Alright, I'll give you a call once the papers are ready and you can open it up."

So Ed had given him the check, waited what seemed like two months, maybe longer, but received no call.

Ed knew that his check hadn't been cashed, but still he had received no call.

Suddenly one day when Ed could stand the wait no longer, Ed called and said, "Charles, what's going on? I mean after all it's a long time. I thought you were going to call me."

"Ed you and I have to talk. I was going to call you but, in the meantime something happened. I cannot give you a lease."

"Why?"

"Because I sold the building to Bank of America."

Ed went immediately to meet with Charles and said, "Charles, it's all right, but what happened?."

"Ed, here is the check, I didn't cash it. I'm sorry, Ed but I just cant."

"All right. All right," and Ed walked out.

When Ed told his attorney what had transpired he said to Ed, "We can put a lawsuit on him for the amount of the lease, because he accepted your check and kept it for a long period of time."

Ed said, "I don't know him that well, but his brother is a good friend of mine. I'm not suing a friend, or even a brother of a friend."

So, Ed went home and stayed away from Charles for two or three weeks. Shortly thereafter, Charles called Ed up and said, "Eddie, I have to talk to you again."

By now, Ed was over it, but Ed said, "Ok where and when?"

Charles responded,"Come down to the office and I'll explain everything."

When Ed saw Charles again that same day Charles began talking before Ed had a chance to ask any questions.

"Eddie, I couldn't give you a lease, but I can tell you now that I am able to stay in the building for five or ten years, before they tear it down."

"Are you sure? And, what does that mean to me?"

"Yes, it's for sure," Charles said. "B of A is planning on rebuilding in that same area, but won't do anything for a long time. So, before they start tearing down anything I want to ask you if you still want to open it up?"

Ed said, "I think yes, but first how much rent do you want?"

"How much to you want to pay?"

Ed said "500, 550 a month".

He said "Forget it! I'm going to tell you how much I want."

Ed said, "Fine, all right, go ahead." Ed expected the worst, but Charles said, "You give me $200 per month. How does that sound?"

Ed was shocked but knew that opportunities like this needed to be acted on immediately. Without any thought Ed cheered, "Ok it's a deal!"

Charles went right to work, "Okay you start fixing it up, hire the people you need, and open it up."

Ed realized shortly thereafter that once again he'd fallen into good fortune. For the first couple months Ed went about the business of starting up a restaurant, never questioning the lack of expenses. Then, he realized that Charles was also paying all the electric and gas bills for the restaurant as part of the whole buildings account. Ed stayed there for 8 years, before Bank of America (originally the Bank of Italy, created during the Depression to help immigrants get a new start in life) followed through with their plan to sell the building.

***

In their restaurant Ed served cocktails to all the executives who were came by daily. All the big guys from the banks, IBM , United Steel, Douglas Oil, etc. frequented the very classy place.

On one side of the lobby of the hotel was the cocktail bar restaurant with a couple of gas torches outside burning. On the other side there was a trophy store which closed down. So Ed called up Charles and asked him "what do you want for that store?" because Ed didn't want someone else coming in with another food operation. He said "uhhh, give me $200 per month." So Eddy paid him for that side.

Eddy made a deli out of it. He opened it because the construction workers across the street came into the Chez, and sometimes had skirmishes with the his regular customers. By opening the deli, he was able to control the situation by making sandwiches and delivering across the street. Ed used to prepare everything on one side of the kitchen and a special deli man (George) ran the deli. It was so busy, he had to hire 3 more young men to make nothing but deliveries for the construction workers and attorney firms who ordered platters of food and pastries. There were lines for sandwiches about a 1/2 block long. They stayed there for 6 years before they tore the building down.

***

One day Eddy got a call about the Redwood House which was kitty corner from the Times building down on 2nd street from one of his waitresses "Eddy this place is going out, called The Redwood House, come and have a look." It was a beautiful place, so Ed put in a bid for the redwood House at $52,000, stainless steel kitchen, walk in refrigerator, anyways very classy. All the reporters from the Times would come into that place. Tom Bradley used to come in. The Mayor of LA. A lot of judges and attorneys, anyways another person put in a bid for $75,000 and the judge knew how Eddy operated and gave it to him for $52,000, so Eddy put down $30,000 for the place and $22,000 note, right, and what happened is, the union came and Ed had experience with the Union. So the Union came and said simply,"Ed, sign this contract."

Ed said, "Wait a minute! It's not sold yet; don't rush it."

Ed knew why the people before him had gone bankrupt. It's because they had to hire extra people because they were so busy lunchtime but in the afternoon nothing. So Eddy wanted to put into the contract that he can hire part-time one or two part-time during lunchtime.

"That's fair, I think, right?"

The Union guy said, "You sign this paper or we'll run you out of town."

Eddy said, "Get the hell out of here!" So he kicked them out and they put a picket line on his place. They picketed for a long time but, in the meantime, Eddy knew what he was doing.

Eddy lost about 40% of his business, but his expenses were covered. Anyway there was an old bartender who worked at that place for a long time and he had a friend and attorney and they came in and said, "Eddy, they want to buy you out. They'll pay what you paid."

Ode to Life!

"No thank you," was Eddy's response. Every few months they came back and offered a little better price. Finally, in about ten months they came back and said, "Look Eddy, I'll give you $100,000."

They told Eddy they wanted to get into the restaurant and cocktail bar business.

"I'll give you $100,000 and they will take over the note the $32000 right and give you for the inventory."

Eddy said, "I'll let you know, but I have to talk to Eveline about it first."

They had a picket line for six or seven months but Eddy wouldn't give in until finally he said, "You know you are an attorney and you are a bar man. Now you are not a restaurant man and he is not a restaurant man, he is a bartender, he thinks he is but he is not."

Eddy wanted no notes, cash on the line.

They said, "It's a deal!" By the time they paid Eddy off, Eddy got out $150,000 with the inventory. He had only put $30,000 down payment on the place.

He had it for a year then sold it to these guys. Ed warned, "You guys will go bankrupt." They did.

They said "Eddy, please stay with us for an extra month and we'll pay you to run the place so we can learn what you know." They wanted Eddy to teach them how to buy, sell, and everything.

Eddy did stay, but the guys, couldn't do it. It was 1966 and Eddy was 38 years old at the time.

***

as told to Gordon Richiusa

The bartender's brother--whom Eddy had no idea about--was one of the big honchos in Philly, a big union official. He was channeling money into the restaurant. But about 3 , 4 years later, they had to close up. Eddy thought that the brother, you know got in trouble. The landlord called him up and said "You know what Ed, when I gave you the lease it was for 10 years, and you are still on it. You come back and take over the restaurant." Eddy said they didn't want to start again with the Union Eddy told the The landlord sold the place.

Eddy was fairly successful and even with the union strike he made a living and had no problems. Even so, about 40% of Eddy's business was gone because a lot of judges didn't want to take sides against the union. Eddy understood that. There were also quite a few attorneys who were union attorneys who also did not or could not cross a picket line.

Eddy had a big clientele from the LA Times, all the reporters every night. Most of them didn't want to close it either. But Eddy had some very good friends. You know across from Jonathan club, across the street? The two twin Bank of America Towers. So Eddy had quite a few customers from there because a lot of big attorneys worked in those buildings.. As a matter of fact, some of the attorneys donated a whole weekend to go to court to force the Union to allow only the limited service of two employees when picketing.

Ode to Life!

Eddy had 4 employees, but had experience with the union because back in NY when Eddy became a Furrier they made him shop chairman and they asked him to be on the executive board of the local AFL/CIO Fur Workers Union. However, Eddy realized in short order how crooked most of them were. Luckily they moved from NY. and came to L.A. via San Francisco. So Eddy knew how the Union worked fairly well.

***

Eddy said to Eveline, "Let's go on vacation first."

He then asked the landlord to put in the necessary paper work so they could try and sell the place.

Eddy didn't want to come back and take over a failing business, even though he could have done it for nothing.

"Alright," the landlord said.

The landlord had an office in the same building on the other side and the Unions had those signs and everything and he told the Union, "Guys, you keep them in Eddy's room over here. The Landlord said for them to keep the signs there overnight and then in the morning they would be ready.

So you could say that he was real partial to the Union, but Eddy didn't want to fight anymore. Eddy could have taken him to court but just didn't. When Eddy got into that business he had put down $30,000 cash in the Redwood House with $22,000 note to the courts and Eddy paid them every month. But when Eddy sold the place, the attorney finally came to him and said "Look Eddy, I will give you a deal. I'll give you $100,000 and you can take over the note and I'll buy the inventory."

***

The entire inventory was given for only $15,000 so Eddy figured a year ago Eddy put in $30,000 and now Eddy could get out with $110,000 or $115,000 *profit* which was a lot back then. So they decided to come back and look for a type of operation which they wouldn't have to work during the weekend.

***

That's how they decided to go into the implant cafeteria business. That's when a big factory lets you feed the employees in their cafeteria. Minimally they have 600 people up to 1000, 1200, 1300. In a big factory in LA. Eddy owned a big cafeteria. The weekends were off as well as holidays. The first one Ed bought was called Proto Tool Company, so what they did is, give him a monthly check like a subsidy to try and keep prices down and give good service. The amount of the subsidy was $750 per month number one. Number two they didn't charge Eddy rent, electric and telephone, no gas bill no nothing.

If and when anything broke down the company fixed it and Eddy had around ten or twelve vending machines, which for some would have been a business unto itself.

Eddy could close at 4 pm but during the workday he had a virtual monopoly for the 800 people working at Proto Tool. Meanwhile another place opened up and a business

Ode to Life!

agent contacted Eddy and said "Eddy you want to buy it? It's very good."

So Eddy and Eveline bought a second business of the same type inside *Tridair Corp*. They had two companies combined together and they had about 1,200 people working there. Over there they said "Look Eddy we want you to make a profit, the company is going to buy a cup of coffee for every employee every morning."

If the employee didn't drink coffee, Eddy gave them a discount on other items. In addition, the company had all kind of parties. Every month Eddy was getting reimbursed as well as not having to pay for utilities or rent. The only expenses were salaries for one cook, two girls to work the counters and serve, and one guy, an older Mexican gentleman Eddy had hired to clean up and fill vending machines.

Eddy ran one site and Eveline ran the other. They moved from Beverly Hills to Rolling Hills because Eddy and Eveline's son David had a breathing problem. They bought a house in Rolling Hills Estates, Palos Verdes, on the coast of California nearby. The sea breezes would probably help clean the air. They were right.

The doctor had told the Hoffmans, "As long as you live here in L.A., your son will have breathing problems." So they went and sold the house and reasoned that the business was close to Rolling Hills. That's when Eddy and Eveline decided to sell the Proto Tool business.

***

Eddy's attorney knew his client well, and knew Eddy wouldn't cheat anybody. Eddy believed in honesty and straight forward business operations, and didn't like to feel he was taking advantage of others. When Eddy was in business he never soaked the people (as he called it). When customers came in...Eddy used to give them extra, always!

That's why he did ok in business, because the customer recognized that they were being given more than what was usually expected. Like when Eddy owned his restaurants he never charged for hors d'oeuvres.

Eddy had two busboys working for him, and all they did was serve free hors d'oeuvres to the tables.

There were pigs-in-a-blanket, miniature cheese burgers, homemade potato chips, little things like that on everyone's plates. This made the customers WANT to purchase drinks!

By now, Eddy and Eveline had two cafeterias going at the same time. Tridair Corporation they owned for 18 years.

Ode to Life!

as told to Gordon Richiusa

Chapter Eleven
Because It Is Healing

E veline became the top consultant for Jenny Craig on the west coast. After she herself had lost 50 pounds on the program, people said they could relate to her. She had many success stories and made many friends through the company. After losing all the weight she put on during and after her last pregnancy, she was feeling so much healthier, happier and in control.

***

Eddy had spent much of his life looking to the next horizon but now he was retired. He found himself with something he never really had before: Free time.

The more time he had to himself, the more he realized that he needed to learn and do new things. He decided to go to Beverly Hills High Night School where he took classes in clay sculpting.

While the female teacher liked Eddy's work, Eddy didn't. Eddys teacher had Czechoslovakian parents. She took a special interest in Eddy, but after one semester Eddy decided to try something else. He also decided to keep two of the pieces that he'd sculpted during that period of time. One was a sculpture he made using a live model (torn ear from an earring) and the other was inspired by the show of

Ode to Life!

CATS. A third piece Ed created a mother and child produced directly from his imagination. That piece still sits above the fireplace mantel in the Hoffman's manor.

Ironically, cats seemed to be attracted to the Hoffman's but Eddy was not a big fan. More than once a cat adopted one of the children and they thought that meant that they could keep it, even if it was technically wild.

Eddy recalled one choice Father's Days where a cat had been taken "back home" and left behind a grocery store, "where it would find the rest of its family," Eddy told the children. One day, while visiting Eddy's cousin Toby (who lived in the Fairfax area and whose husband, Jack had worked in a butcher shop there near Fairfax and 3rd street) Toby was putting food out for another feral cat that turned out to be the same cat that Eddy had dropped off!

***

In a much later incident later, Suzanne was shopping at a Sketcher's outlet. An older woman and her husband were there, shopping for their granddaughter. "Which one of these do you think a little girl would like best? the woman struck up a conversation.

"They're both nice," Suzanne answered politely.

She was there to buy Hanukkah gifts for her nephews and said as much to the woman. This opened the door to additional conversation and details about being Jewish (as they all were) as well as Suzanne being late for the Hanukkah party. Suzanne also mentioned that she did not want to be late for her father's brisket.

This led the woman to tell Suzanne that she and her husband had owned a kosher butcher shop in Fairfax, as well. After further conversation--the checkout line was long at Sketchers that day--it turns out that the butcher shop was the same shop where Jack had worked years before! Suzanne believed that her father had a special power, a penchant for intersecting his life with others.

***

The Hoffman family did have pets, usually dogs including a German Shepherd named Snoopy, named by David and a toy poodle (some said cockapoo) named Perky.

Perky knew a lot of tricks and was very smart, but couldn't keep up with the children. "Hey Perky," one of them would say to impress visitors, "Go get your leash" and Perky would run to the laundry room and pull her leash off a peg where it was kept, carrying it to the kids. The "trick" was on Perky most of the time, as the children rarely took her for a walk at that time.

Another trick that she could do was "smile" on command, which meant that she would lift her top lip to the point that it would make Perky sneeze. They could just as easily have said, "Perky, sneeze!"

When Eddy and Eveline had The Chez a woman who ran the hotel had a dog that she needed to get rid of. That was how the Hoffmans got Perky. Perky had a boyfriend too. A neighbor's black poodle that would drive Perky crazy every time he and the owner walked by. The Hoffmans even allowed this canine suitor a chance to rendezvous in their backyard on occasion. Luckily, or unluckily depending upon who you asked, no puppies resulted from these trysts.

Perky and Snoopy moved with the family to Palos Verdes. Early on when the Hoffmans first moved there, Perky and Snoopy got out onto the front street. Luckily, it was a cul de sac. Perky sat on the front porch and started barking to Snoopy to come back. Snoopy was running up the street and onto the busy main street, Silver Spur. Snoopy didn't listen and ended up getting hit by a car. The neighbor, Isabel saw this and called the SPCA to come pick up Snoopy before the kids got home.

Eddy also became active in Cub Scouts and then Boy Scouts with both his sons. He also took all the kids to the Malibu Pier many times. The trips usually culminated in some sort of fish story.

On one trip, before Eddy and his sons had reached PCH, it started to rain. He took a look out the side window, then up at the sky through the windshield, as if assessing the situation.

"Boys, I'm sorry but we have to give up fishing for today. "

"Why?"

"Well, it looks like it's going to rain for a while and the fish won't bite on a day like this."

"Why? Are they afraid of clouds?"

"No, fish just don't like to get wet," Ed said without expression.

The boys never blinked because they believed him. There was no ill-intent on Eddy's part; his actions proving time again the old adage: You Mostly Tease The Ones You Love.

Eddy and Eveline always put the well-being of their children above all else. Cub Scouts, Girl Scouts and Boy Scouts found the two parents volunteering as troop co-leaders, beyond and above their usual duties, always with humor and a playful attitude.

***

On a different adventure, different day, at the same pier in Malibu, daughter Suzanne had asked to go along. She never even touched a fishing pole and lost interest quickly. There was very little to do at the end of the pier except fish though. So periodically she would check a bucket of water where the day's catch would be kept, to keep them fresh. Several times she came to the bucket and it was empty, but on one trip she saw one fish that her dad had caught and placed there. The fish had died and was floating sideways at the surface of the bucket. Suzanne made sure the fish was dead by poking it a couple of times, and then decided to throw it back into the ocean.

"Let's go home," Eddy said when he realized what had become of their efforts.

***

While living in Laguna Woods Village, Ed found out that there was a group called Honor Flights of San Diego. Through them, he was invited, free of charge, to go to

Washington D.C. for a weekend with other major war veterans, including those who served in World Wars, Vietnam, and Korea.

The honored veterans were all pushed around in wheel chairs by volunteers who had paid for the privilege of being their caretaker for the weekend. Eddy had a Pentagon captain who wheeled him around and who become very fond of Eddy.

In fact, he made Eddy a Honorary Navy Captain and gave him a medallion that stated as much.

"I want to honor you and give you this," he said handing Eddy the medal.

"But I wasn't even in the Navy," Eddy protested mildly.

"You deserve it anyway."

This captain had found out that Eddy was Military Intelligence, while pushing Eddy around in the wheelchair he'd asked Eddy details of his experience.

"Softening up with artillery shells was not enough on V-Day," Eddy had said, adding, "The enemy was too heavily barricaded. Why didn't they start with Gasoline? I would rather that they be burned alive than our people."

Eddy had given this some thought. He knew that many more lives would have been saved if the Allies had destroyed these bunkers. Gasoline seemed the logical weapon of choice, as it would have made these bunkers inoperable from the outset. The Pentagon captain agreed and wondered why Eddy hadn't stayed in the military.

One of Eddy's cousins—his mother's side—who had visited him in Japan, was a full-bird colonel. He had asked Eddy to, "Please stay in the military!"

However, Eddy did not see himself staying in the military as a career. "I think I can have a better life if I retire as soon as my tour ends."

Later, this same cousin also had retired and wanted Eddy to open an optometry office with him in Long Island, but since Eddy had no experience and other interests, he moved in a different direction. Also, if he had stayed in Long Island, he would probably not ever have met Eveline.

Eddy flew first class home. When he arrived at the San Diego airport he found his daughter, Carla and her two sons, Colin and Canyon, there waiting to greet him. The lobby was packed with well wishers all holding American flags.

***

Eveline had finally come to grips with her past and often over the years this special couple were asked to speak about their experiences during The Holocaust. While they tried never to turn down a request, their favorite audience could be found at middle schools.

Many of these kids were the same age Ed was when he was taken to Auschwitz. As more and more kids heard Eveline and Ed were coming to speak, the numbers in the group—kids, parents, and teachers—always grew. Many times though an auditorium would have made seating more comfortable, the Hoffmans preferred the intimacy of having over 200 kids sitting on a floor mesmerized.

Ed and Eveline never used a script. They just spoke from their hearts. Usually, the time was limited by the regular schedule, but always after the usual forty minutes to an hour that was allotted, there were so many questions most of them went unanswered.

Eveline realized that their talks had lasting effect when soon after, the Hoffmans began receiving letters, hundreds, thanking them for sharing their story. Young, old, and in between told the two Holocaust Survivors that their stories had affected them deeply. The last time they spoke was at a gathering in 2019. It took so much energy, especially from Ed that health considerations took precedence. Here are some samples of letters (many from middle school students) who had been personally affected by the Hoffmans' stories over the five decades where they had shared their stories:

"Dear Mr. Hoffman,

Firstly, thank you so much for speaking about your experience during the Holocaust to me and my peers. It was truly a gift to hear your life story, and I will remember it for the rest of my life.

Secondly, thank you for sharing some of your wisdom with us. The second you started to tell your story, the whole room was mesmerized. Your stories about all your different experiences were incredibly brave; you are such an inspiration.

Finally, I just wanted to let you know that I honestly believe that you bestowed a gift upon us, that we should be grateful to have learned. When my friend, [M] asked you if you hated the Nazis for what they had done to you, you said that you didn't hate them because, at the end of the day, nobody cares if you hate someone else, so why waste your energy on that when you could use it on happier things. I think that is one of the wisest things I have ever heard. It really helped me in my own life; I now always try to love instead of hate. I cannot thank you enough for sharing that with me.

"...Everything you said made me understand how horrible the Nazis were and all the arduous tasks you had to complete just to stay alive. For instance, when you worked in the coal mine, I don't think that I would ever be able to do the amount of forced labor, just as you did, AND with a lack of supplies. Very admirable. When you explained how you were strapped to a table and had your appendix taken out, I got chills and realized that no matter how tough things may get, if you have the mentality "mind over matter" you will survive.

"...Your speech educated me by telling me what people are capable of doing to other people and to not be mean to other people because of their religion or race. Your speech

Ode to Life!

impacted me because I now know how one person can change billions of lives. you speech changed me because now I know how not to take my friends and family for granted and to be grateful for the things I have.

"Mr. and Mrs. Hoffman,
...The way that you were able to keep your faith and not doubt it was really amazing. The Holocaust shows what can happen when people want power so badly. I think this is a very important thing to learn about what happened in history. This will [help] this generation and generations to come to not repeat the past. You are truly changing the world with your story. Thank you for the impact that you have made! I will never forget this amazing story and the terrors of the Holocaust."

***

Because of their pasts, Eddy and Eveline as with all parents, had learned to apply what they could from their stories as lessons to their own children about how people function in the the modern world. Interestingly, many of these lessons revolved around automobiles.

The Hoffman family had a Toyota Corona, what Eveline felt was a great car that had belonged to her. Ed drove a Suburban but Eveline had this other car because she drove a fair distance to work and the Corona definitely got better gas mileage than the Suburban.

Ed had planned "unofficially" to share his car with Suzanne knowing that because she decided to stay at Beverly Hills High to graduate and was planning on attending Humbolt State--about 650 miles away--her need was the greatest.

Suzanne had also expressed a future consideration, "What am I going to do for a car when I come back from college?" she asked.

***

Before Suzanne left for college, she took her turn shopping for the family at the local grocery store. To this day there is still a debate about who's dollar it was but that amount was about all that was left over from the grocery money that Suzanne's dad claimed her father had given her.

Suzanne says that she had her own dollar. Eddy says that if he knew what would transpire he would gladly have given an extra dollar to his daughter.

Regardless what happened is this: While at the market, Suzanne was approached by a boy selling raffle tickets for Children's Hospital. There was going to be a raffle later at the Portuguese Bend Horse Show. Suzanne felt like it was fate that she could give away her last dollar to such a worthy cause. She agreed to buy one ticket (all she could afford). Out of 5000 tickets sold, Suzanne's turned out to be the winner. Her prize was a Toyota Corolla stick-shift.

Of course, Suzanne had learned to drive in her mom's automatic Toyota so she had to ask a friend who was already in College and who owned a Volkswagen Bug to teach her how to drive a stick. These early Beetles also had another quirk as the gearbox put *reverse* in the opposite direction of most other cars. This caused a slight concern for Suzanne but overall she was starting to believe in a special Hoffman Luck, a providence that seemed to look over the family members as they tried to be their own best examples.

***

When Suzanne did finally leave for college at Humboldt State University in Northern California, one of her first professors was teaching cultural studies. This professor, she found out was a Holocaust survivor himself, and he was studying why people were altruistic, or put themselves in danger to hide others during WWII.

His name was Professor Samuel Olner. He also lectured in various other locations in California. Dr. Olner told Suzanne about a lecture that he was giving at Cal State Fullerton in Southern California. After discussing her teacher with her father, he mentioned that there had been an Olner with them in England. Eddy and Eveline decided to go see him lecture. Eddy brought his memory book from England and turned to a page with all the kids. Dr. Olner looked at it and said, "I remember that kid. We played soccer on opposite teams.He knocked me down and was so apologetic when he helped me up." Of course, the image that Dr. Olner was pointing out was Eddy.

***

Eveline was still working for Jenny Craig in San Pedro when she and Ed moved to Laguna Woods Village. This senior community had been spawned from the original Leisure World organization and would play heavily into both Eddy and Eveline's future enjoyment. At this time, Eveline wasn't ready to fully retire so asked for a transfer to the local Jenny Craig store in Laguna Niguel. She was promptly transferred and started a successful career there.

***

In the senior village where the Hoffmans still reside, the clubs covered every interest from Archery to Video Production. One such club is The Korean American Club. Every year this club honors all Korean War Veterans. Eddy has been honored each year for several years now. It is always a big affair. Eddy says that he can feel the gratitude for the support the U.S. military gave to the Korean and descendants of Korean people during that war. Pictures were taken, and Eddy was interviewed and spoke to the group. They had given him gifts and hugged him in years past, but no hugs this year because the Coronavirus threat was just starting.

Eveline and Eddy both felt that these were a wonderfully appreciative audience. As an example of this, all the honored guests were gifted with a stylish camouflage hunting vest with an embroidered symbols for both the Korean War Veterans, and combination Korean and U.S. Flag with the words, "Let's Go Together."

After speaking, Eddy ended up answering the usual questions. Eddy's story needed no embellishment and he tried several times to correct his hosts when they asked him about particular cities or battles that took place on their cultural continent. "I was never in Korea," he started off saying simply, but soon gave up trying to explain that he never actually served IN Korea during this war. "I was in Military Intelligence and assigned to a different location."

This message never got through and after being asked several dozen times to comment on specific locations inside of Korea, Eddy finally resigned himself to say, "It's a wonderful country with wonderful people. I like them all."

***

In 1987 Eveline learned that she'd developed breast cancer in one of her breasts.

"Their is no sign of cancer in both breasts, but you have options," she remembers the doctor telling her.

One option was less invasive than the other called a lumpectomy.

"What's my other option?" She asked her doctor after careful consideration.

In the end, Eveline opted for the second option, a mastectomy. She wanted the *devil* out of her and did not want to have to deal with any ongoing reoccurrences. Many friends and family had opinions about Eveline's decision, but as was her nature, when she made up her mind, that was the end of the discussion. Eddy supported Eveline, as usual, in her decision.

After the surgery to remove her right breast Eveline had reconstructive surgery, and did really well after that. No reoccurrences were ever detected. Eddy was by her side at every stage, including the counseling sessions prior to surgery and the decision to do the mastectomy.

"No one will ever know the difference unless you tell them," he had said.

***

Then in early 2010 Eveline was struck by another disease, Multiple Myeloma, a type of plasma cell cancer. The later part of 2010, Arlene Detwiler a good friend wanted to do a "special" party. She called it "A Pre Bone Marrow Transplant Party." Only women were invited to witness the shaving of the head. All of the women who were invited (at least 20) came to the event. Many brought gifts of scarves. Eveline's head was shaved by another friend, Laurie (a hairdresser), because Eveline knew that she would be loosing her hair and wanted to stay ahead of that.

When the last hair was gone, one male *did* crash the party. Eddy showed up with his head shaved in solidarity with his wife.

Eveline was shocked, but she noticed that the bald-man who had just crashed the party had a familiar, wry grin.

Eddy wanted to surprise his wife, but he knew that eventually both heads would be covered with hair again.

"Surprise!" was all he said.

***

One friend gave a card that was in French that said,
"C*hère Eveline,*
Vous serez très belle avec votre crâne rasé. Nous vous souhaitons une récupération rapide après votre énorme opération. Vous avez beaucoup de courage et de force, ce qui est nécessaire. Nous vous souhaitons également bonne chance. Nos pensées et nos sentiments sincères vous accompagnent."
Bisous, Susan et David

The English translation is: "You will be very beautiful with your shaved head. We wish you a fast recovery after your enormous operation. You have a lot of courage and strength, which is needed. We also wish you luck. Our thoughts and heartfelt sentiments are with you."
— Kisses, Susan and David

***

Two other friends, Odette and Ellen wrote Odes.
Ellen wrote: **ODE TO EVELINE**
An ode to Eveline, the fair
Soon to be bereft of hair
For you, 'twill be a piece of cake
for hair does not the woman make.
Think not what's missing from your head
Think just of what you'll gain instead
You will not have a "bad hair" day
Nor need to cover up the gray.
There'll be no stubborn hairy dome

as told to Gordon Richiusa

To battle daily with a comb
Nor thoughts of something diabolical
To change each wayward hairy follicle
Away with costly hair salon
With stylists to depend upon
All potions, lotions, sprays you'll waive
Just think of all the bucks you'll save!
For lustrous locks, however dyed
Cannot compare with what's inside
And beauteous hair, whatever length
Will never match your inner strength
What truly makes a lady fair
Does not depend upon her hair
And with your charm and winning ways
You just might start a "no hair" craze.
--With Love and Good Vibrations,
Ellen

Odette's was called,
ODE TO HAIR.
Hair's like air...it's everywhere!
On your head, in the bed,
In the bath, on the chair,
Hair is everywhere.
Have you found it on your chin?
Nose hairs are another thing!
And around the lips it's fun,
Or tucked inside your favorite bun.

Ode to Life!

Legs and armpits, bikini line,
Tweezer's out, let's hear you whine.
Hair's a pain, let's all admit it.
One of us is going to quit it.
No more color, no more goo,
Shave it off and start anew.
Bald and skinny, rub for luck,
(Looks a bit like Friar Tuck!)
Not to worry, it'll grow.
You'll be back to wash and blow.
In the meantime, hats are in.
Wigs can work if that's your thing.
Bald or hairy, plump or lean,
You are still our Eveline.
Fight the fight and hurry home.
We'll be waiting...with a comb.
--With much Love, Odette

***

From her years with Jenny Craig, Eveline had learned good nutrition habits; she learned exactly what she could eat and how much. Paying close attention to her weight also prevented either skyrocket gains or unhealthy, rapid losses. She felt like she was in control and could look to the future. Ironically, when she had lost fifty pounds she realized that this loss made her feel whole again. She was often happy, satisfied, especially when she was with her husband or children, but feeling whole, like that emptiness she once visualized as a child in the orphanage and her second foster home was finally filled with the light of love. She loved her family and they loved her, but she also realized that she loved herself. It didn't matter how this transformation took place. She was not afraid to mention her therapy sessions that began after her incident at the Child Survivors of Los Angeles meeting. She was happy, and she knew it. That's what mattered most.

Eveline realized that by having four children, and being active with them had been a blessing in her transformation. As pounds fell off she could keep up with her kids easier. In fact, she noticed that every movement was easier and easier the less weight she had to carry. So, when she lost the weight, she kept it off.

Like anyone, she might make an occasional late night raid on the fridge, but that only led to her limiting the next day's calorie intake--something not always easy when one lives with an excellent baker.

Growing up, her children said they never felt any pressure when it came to food and eating, because their father continued to produce delicious home cooked masterpieces at most meals, and of course his specialty was desserts. No one in the family, including Eveline ever said *no* to one of Eddy's creations.

Eddy never had the same overeating obsession that plagued his wife, but because of his being starved for almost two years in the camps, growing up in the food industry, also owning restaurants and cooking for battalions of hungry soldiers, he tended to buy a lot of food.

It made him feel at home keeping his cupboards and other storage areas full to the maximum at all times. If he had a weakness it was that he felt he needed to have food readily available at all times.

Just after getting liberated, Eddy may have started eating more than he was used to, because he could eat whenever he wanted. After that it was enough to simply have food available. He rarely cooked just for himself, however.

***

Settling into life in Laguna Woods, Eddy heard about the arts and crafts building. So, he went down to check out the jewelry lab there.

"That's something I always wished I had learned more about," he told Eveline.

A few days later he walked into the class, into the lab telling the supervisor that he wanted to learn how to work with jewelry. The class supervisor was a guy named Murray who was in charge. A woman named Jan, Murray's wife ran the glasswork class.

All new students were asked to contribute $20 to pay for raw materials.

Eddy wrote a check instantly and went to work, but as soon as Murray saw the first thing Eddy did, he tore up the check.

"Why?" Eddy asked, seeing what Murray had done.

"I don't know how I got so lucky to have you think you should enter this class, but obviously you don't need me," Murray said. "In fact, you should think about becoming the supervisor here some day." That's how Eddy started working in the Jewelry Shop, and led to another example of people wanting to reward Eddy in some way.

People were always trying to give Eddy something, or to get him involved in their schemes.

Another supervisor, a man named McHenry who had been a veterinarian in his day-job, had problems with leukemia for 18 years. McHenry liked Eddy because the both of them had grown up in an orphanage.

McHenry's wife was named Evelyn, and though her name was pronounced differently than Eveline, with a different spelling the bonds were strengthened.

Evelyn was a hoarder. This affliction seemed to affect both McHenry (to some degree) and his wife, forcing McHenry not to notice that much of the clutter in their home was actually equipment that *he* was using to make Jewelry. There was always a plan on moving into or out of the Jewelry Shop this bulky and expensive equipment. So, turning a blind eye on himself, he decided that what really annoyed him was his *wife's* clutter. McHenry's solution to the problem made Ed smile.

Instead of working on changing the wife's bad habits, McHenry decided to buy her a second house of her own in the same community. Escrow was easy, so shortly thereafter, he moved her and her stacks of clutter out of their joint dwelling and immediately set to the task of finding room for his own equipment.

Everything McHenry did he felt compelled to share his thinking in detail to Eddy in advance. This maneuver gave the appearance of him seeking council and advice *before* making a decision. However, McHenry rarely actually followed Ed's advice, but the two spent time together, as Eddy would cook for McHenry on a weekly basis.

McHenry had provided a 24 hour caregiver for his wife when Evelyn had become mostly unable to perform daily tasks. The caregiver was a woman from Guatemala, and was basically 100% responsible for the wife, before, during, and even after the move.

***

When Les McHenry's wife knew she was dying, she wanted her husband to promise her that he would take care of her caregiver's finances after she passed. So he opened up a 2,000,000 account in the caregiver's name so she could get five percent interest a year.

By this time, McHenry was getting sicker and sicker, himself. "Eddy I have decided to marry the caregiver so that I could leave all my money (14 million) to Felicia, and not not just give it all to the state of California.

"If I were you," Eddy said. "Instead of marrying her, leave some money to the Vets, to the Laguna Woods Foundation and spread it around."

"You're absolutely right," McHenry had said, promising he would take Eddy's advice.

(Another friend) Nina Colbert told Eddy, "You are in the will, you'll see."

After McHenry passed away, his executor Nina told Eddy that he also was in Les's will. Eddy found out that the caregiver Felicia had been given an *additional $10 million*. The rest went to The Laguna Woods Foundation, American Veterans and others.

Eddy inherited all of Les's jewelry equipment, most of which Eddy donated to the Jewelry Shop.

He left Eddy a little money as well. It was the least that one orphan could do for another.

***

Another friend wanted to buy Eddy a car. Eddy was always driving him around.

"Come on Eddy. What kind of car do you want?"

"Stop it! You are not buying me a car!"

"Do you like the new Cadillacs?" he went on, undeterred.

"You're not buying me a car or anything else!" Eddy was emphatic. His name was Ed Markowitz.

***

By this time, Eveline had come to grips with her childhood traumas and decided that it was time to relax, maybe try some of the things she had been afraid to before now. She heard about a class that piqued her interest. A woman named Jeannie Sanner had an actors studio before she retired and was offering a class free of charge in the senior village. The only acting Eveline had done was a role in Anton Chekov's Marriage Proposal. Her sister Jacqueline directed her in San Francisco at a theater she was involved in.

"I think I will take that class," she said to Eddy, who encouraged his wife to fulfill her dream of acting.

The first real opportunity she had to act was when she was picked for a scene where she would play a very common young woman who was applying for a companionship job to a wealthy classy older woman. The older character was performed by Shirley MacLaine on the big screen. Eveline really appreciated having Jeannie as a director. She thought very highly of her teaching methods. The president of Old Pros, Sheila Bialka at the time, came in to see how well the new actors were doing in the class and she picked four of them out of twelve to perform at an Old Pros meeting, including Eveline.

Shortly thereafter Sheila Bialka was directing a production called "45 Seconds From Broadway". Eveline approached her and asked, in a completely uncharacteristic manner, "Do you think you could find a small part for me?"

"Absolutely," Sheila said

Eveline got one of the leads.

Every time there was a new production Eveline got a good role. A lot of memorizing, a lot of work. "But I loved it, because I could become the person I was portraying. The best part of the whole experience was the reaction of the audience."

"It was a wonderful thing," she said, to know that what she did made people happy.

Eddy asked Eveline once, "Were you acting when we first got married?"

"For me to know and you to find out," she said.

Eveline's sister had been a director at a small theater company when she lived in San Francisco. This may have helped spawn Eveline's interest in acting.

Her mother had so wanted to be an actress, but her parents wouldn't allow it. She was often called *Sarah Bernhardt*.

She was very beautiful.

***

"When Eddy lived in London, his landlady's daughter, a 13 year old had developed a huge crush on Eddy." She came to visit as an adult when Eddy and Eveline had moved to Rolling Hills Estates. She came to the U.S. with husband, sister, mother and father and told Eddy how much she LOVED him when she was a girl. Eddy had promised to send her bubblegum when he had left London to America. She never forgot it and was very disappointed when the bubblegum never arrived. When Eddy had known this girl, she was exactly the same age as Eveline (at the time).

***

Ode to Life!

Eddy enjoyed working with friends and students, and was always helping everyone. Sometimes Eddy spent his own money repairing other people's jewelry and just liked the feeling of accomplishment and joy this hobby provided. One day a guy named Gordon came into the Jewelry shop and spotted Eddy.

"Hi, I was told to come here this morning and ask for someone named Eddy. I was told that he might be able to help me with a personal project.

"I'm Eddy. What is the project?"

The previous day, Gordon had come to the manager of the recreation department with a thin piece of aluminum that had been shaped into a twin-heart design. He said that he was wondering if anyone could help him recreate a replica of this bracelet/bangle and said, "My father was a Pearl Harbor survivor, a marine and he pulled this piece of aluminum off one of the Japanese planes that were shot down December 7, 1941. I'm hoping to make an exact replica of this, but I'm not having much luck."

The clubhouse manager said simply, "Come back in the morning and talk to Eddy. He will be able to help."

The next morning when Gordon returned and told Eddy his story, without hesitation, Eddy Hoffman agreed to help create an exact replica of the Two-Hearts-Beating-As-One or Heroes' Hearts bracelet that Gordon had brought with him. Gordon also had created a paper pattern, traced by hand to replicate the shape.

"Will you be able to use this?"

"I think this will be pretty easy," Eddy said, took the pattern and set straight to work.

While he worked the tiny piece of metal by hand, he told Gordon his story of being in the Death Camps during WWII. Gordon was a journalist and writer and asked if he could come back with an on-camera interviewer to hear the same stories again.

"I'd like to put you on camera and record your story," Gordon said.

"Sure," Eddy said. He didn't mind talking about his experiences and had done so many times. At this point, Gordon didn't know about the video recordings that had been made by the **Children of the Shoah** project done by Steven Spielberg and others. He didn't know that several others had tried to write this story before, or that Eveline Hoffman was also a Holocaust survivor.

Gordon only knew that he didn't want to make the same mistake he'd made with his own parents, waiting until they were gone before acting on what they had to teach. He wasn't sure, but he knew that he'd stumbled onto something important.

After Eddy had fashioned an aluminum bracelet with a unique design Gordon called, "Two-Hearts-Beating-As-One" or "Heroes' Hearts" as he'd dubbed the band of aluminum, Eddy asked permission to make a copper version of the same bracelet and design.

"Why copper?" Gordon asked.

"Because," Eddy said "Copper is healing."

If anyone else had said that to Gordon he probably wouldn't have paid much attention, but coming from Eddy Hoffman, an Auschwitz survivor, well even Gordon could see the importance and significance.

Eddy cut a half-dozen of these handmade copper bracelets and he gave them to Gordon.

A few days later, Gordon returned to the Jewelry shop with a woman named, Michelle Manu, a half-Hawaiian woman with a great on and off camera presence.

Holding a microphone, Michelle sat across a workbench from Eddy while Gordon set up a camera. For the first time Eddy heard someone speak on his behalf, Michelle saying to the camera that Eddy's story had focused the non-profit that Gordon had created to fulfill his promise to his father.

"*As Gordon set out to find a jewelry maker to handmake the Heroes' Hearts bracelet, he ran into a jewelry maker by the name of Eddy Hoffman. Eddy's personal path, and story has affected the Heroes' Hearts direction and we wanted to share it with you now.*"

Turning to Eddy Michelle asked, "*Eddy what was your process in making this prototype?*"

"I help out everybody here," Eddy began. I enjoy doing jewelry and I enjoy experimenting, seeing how far I can go. So, I started making this jewelry. He showed me the pattern and I cut it out myself."

"How do you feel about this prototype?" Michelle pressed.

Eddy smiled a wry smile and said simply, "If it's good for him, it's good for me."

***

There were a series of false starts and obstacles that had to be overcome. In 2017, still trying to determine the best course of action for his non-profit, Gordon tried to honor Eddy Hoffman with what he called an *Aloha Award*, given to those who've done something of significance on behalf of others.

It was supposed to be presented by the Mayor of The City of Laguna Woods during a Veterans Day memorial event conducted inside Laguna Woods Village by a local American Legion post of which Eddy is a member. The flag bearers and honor guard who were the local American Legion troop were given exact replicas of the Heroes' Hearts Bracelet in thanks for their service.

Unfortunately, while Eddy and Eveline were sitting front and center at the event, a local Village MC who did not recognize Eddy, decided not to make any effort to honor Eddy or allow the presentation to be made and refused to make an announcement calling Eddy to the podium. The event ended abruptly, without Eddy receiving the award.

The failed attempt was rectified later in a smaller arguably more significant ceremony that took place at Eddy's beloved Jewelry Shop inside the Laguna Woods Village.

Ode to Life!

This time Gordon made the presentation so that there would be no screw ups.

The more that Gordon learned about Eddy and Eveline's story, the more he realized that "doing something good" would involve these two Holocaust survivors.

Gordon was both a card-carrying journalist and a novelist, editor, and publisher who had brought to life more than one based-on-true-events tale. Naturally his mind moved in that direction. Several others had recorded Eveline and Eddy's stories, and tried to make sense of them. Eveline's sister, Jacqueline had written about the dream and the death camps on behalf of her brother-in-law, but no one had yet taken a step back and made the leap to present the truth as a good old fashioned story.

Gordon approached Eddy and then met with him and Eveline at their home to discuss the possibility of turning their experiences into a novel-based-on-fact through the non-profit that Gordon had founded based upon his father's words to Do Something Good.

Gordon decided to take the copper version of the Two-Hearts-As-One bracelet to Rabbi Cooper at the Los Angeles Museum of Tolerance, if Rabbi Cooper was interested. He was. A special meeting was set and Eddy and Gordon drove from Orange County to Los Angeles (a distance of about 60 miles) to make the presentation.

Things did not go smoothly at first. Gordon and Eddy drove to the rabbi's office on a day where Gordon's navigation application was not working well. Eddy said that he knew where they were going, so Gordon took turn-by-turn directions from Eddy, who said he was familiar with the area. After the Aloha Award ceremony debacle, Gordon hoped that this event would go more smoothly.

That, unfortunately was not the case because Eddy had taken Gordon to the Holocaust Museum, whereas Rabbi Cooper was expecting them at the Museum of Tolerance, about a mile away.

Arriving at the back entrance of the Holocaust Museum Gordon pressed an intercom button and was redirected back to the correct location.

Within that square mile of their destination, Eddy and Gordon became progressively more lost and traffic became more jammed, until it was clear that they had missed their appointment. They called the rabbi and apologized that, "We're going to be a little late."

Luckily, Rabbi Cooper was as tolerant as the Museum's name and through his assistant told Eddy and Gordon that, "Whenever you arrive the rabbi will adjust his schedule to meet with you."

Security was tight, but Eddy and Gordon were expected and led into a waiting area where Rabbi Cooper met the two.

"Thank you for seeing us," Gordon said by way of breaking the ice. "You seem very secure here,' he added, commenting on the security staff who protected the museum and office building.

"Well," said the Rabbi. "Here is the guy who I want to protect me!" He put his left had on Ed's shoulder and shook his guest's hand with his right. "There is nobody who is better equipped or tougher than this guy right here."

He then led the two into his office, where they took some photos, told some stories, and gave the original copper bracelet that Eddy had made from the design of Gordon's father to the rabbi.

The bangle came with a certificate of authenticity and a document awarding the copper bangle "with no strings attached."

Gordon showed the rabbi the original, aluminum bracelet for comparison. "He made these replicas exactly! It's pretty amazing," said Gordon.

***

After the photos, the bracelet was put inside a small, round display container and placed on the massive bookshelf behind the rabbi's desk.

It was like another round of *Six Degrees of Eddy Hoffman*.

The rabbi asked, "So what now?"

"I wanted to ask you your opinion," said Gordon. "I currently have this original on display at the Pacific Island Ethnic Art Museum in Long Beach, but I think there might be something else I should do with it. I started a non-profit and we can now manufacture exact replicas, with the help of the VETS program at Saddleback College. I don't really want to give this artifact to either of the U.S. or Japanese governments, since I feel that the attack at Pearl Harbor involved two imperialistic countries fighting over land that did not belong to either one of them. On the other hand, it seems like something else should be done. I'm wondering if I should give this original back to the Japanese people somehow, or even the descendants of the pilot and crew who were killed in the plane crash where my father got the aluminum."

"No," Eddy interrupted. "I don't think you should give it to either of the governments."

"Me either," said the rabbi. "I think I know some people who might be able to help you find the descendants, if any, but it doesn't seem right to just give it to the government. I'm sure you'll do the right thing."

***

From this meeting, the **Reconciliation Project** was born at Heroes' Hearts Inc and it was decided, with the help of the Park Service at the Arizona Memorial in Hawaii and King Kamehameha's Royal Order to give *copper* bracelets to the Japanese descendants of the killed pilot. These would be awarded by two Holocaust survivors (Eddy and Eveline Hoffman) at a special ceremony that was to include the United Nations.

The original aluminum bracelet had already been given to the Pacific Island Ethnic Art Museum in Long Beach, California. A special ceremony was to take place on or before the 80th Anniversary of the attack on Pearl Harbor.

Ode to Life!

A documentary was begun, spotlighting the historical significances of Indigenous Hawaiian people, Italian and Sicilian Americans, African Americans, Japanese Americans, and the Jewish people who are mostly left out of the story of WWII. The film in progress is called, ***Pieces of Aloha***.

***

Soon after this meeting, Eddy turned 90.

Suzanne, Carla, Joe and David Hoffman wanted to do something special for their father and began planning a big event. They chose one of the venues inside the sprawling senior community called Laguna Woods Village, but worried that the Southern California location would prevent some from attending.

That problem did not materialize. When the clock struck 1 p.m., all banquet tables were filled with Hoffmans. There were not enough seats. At one point in the planning, the children wanted to cancel the party because Eddy had been in the hospital a week before and he wasn't fully recovered.

Eveline also had a bad cold but this was a big milestone and neither would hear of cancelling. They reasoned that people were flying in from out of town, and both of them had been through much worse than a few hours of adulation from their family. A little stay in an actual hospital was nothing to Eddy. In fact, he even decided to bake for his own party. Everybody always loved his biscottis which were actually a recipe that he took from Eveline's niece's husband, Bob (who also attended).

Eveline's niece, Sandy Schlechter flew in from Oakland but Sandy's sister, Nicole was unable to attend. Instead, she ordered huge Happy Birthday balloons for Eddy and Eveline and had them delivered to the banquet room where the party was being held. Had Suzanne known this, she would have not run around looking for helium for the balloons she also had bought, which was in short supply at the time. Sandy had written a poem about Eddy previously which summed up many of the relative's feeling about Eddy.

> Here Sandy's Poem:
> Once upon a time there lived a man
> Who was the greatest Uncle in all the land.
> Folks would come from far and & wide
> To stand in the kitchen by his side,
> To watch split peas & dumplings cook
> They'd come and smell, they'd come and look.
> His potato salad was clean & pure
> With plenty of mayo, to be sure.
> His rugelach cookies were heaven-scent
> To family & friends 'cross the state they went.
> Five hours of brunch was never enough,
> As course after course of dinner they'd stuff
> Of boeuf bourgignon & scampied shrimp
> There was always tons — no need to skimp.

And he'd gladly share all his magic of food,
You could try to recreate it, (but not to be rude).....
NO ONE can cook like my Uncle Ed,
Teller of wild stories & baker of bread.
He has friends, fans & groupies he's never even met
Who MAY grab some cookies, but there's one
 thing they can't get.......
.....When he calls me "sweetheart" and pinches my cheek,
My heart fills with love, and my face hurts for a week!..

***

Carla sang and performed a song she had written just for the occasion. It was a great party.

***

Eddy and Eveline had impacted many individuals throughout their lives—lives that had remained and flourished under the most incredible of circumstances—merely with continued adherence to the policy of being one's own best example.

When they had moved to Laguna Woods they met "one of the oldest living humans in the world" in the same senior community as they were living.

Eddy, still baking for his family, friends, and neighbors began the weekly ritual of bringing one or two loaves of fresh bread to Irv Piken every Tuesday. This lasted for well over a decade.

While there, Eddy and Irv would talk over old times and share stories and commiserate together. The visits sometimes lasted for hours because Eddy felt that listening to this gentleman (who was literally old enough to be his father) was a matter of simple human decency.

"Eddy," Irv would say almost every week, "You're the only person who comes to visit me. My family is mostly all gone and those who are alive are too far away to visit. I'm just not a priority I guess."

***

About a year later, shortly after Eddy's 91st birthday and just before Eveline's 83rd birthday, they got the news that their friend, the 111 year old, had died in his sleep.

The obituary headline read:

Oldest Person Living in the U.S. Dies at 111.

Irving Piken died on a Friday.

It was in all the papers with one picture showing Eveline giving Irv a kiss on the cheek at his most recent birthday party.

***

Two weeks later, the Corona Virus pandemic crippled human activity around the globe and affected changes to our lives on Earth. Many had taken for granted their freedom of movement which we'd all come to appreciate.

Eddy and Eveline were self sequestered in their senior village condo that looked out over a golf course that was also shut down. It was weird to see the ninth hole from their living room window as a quiet grassy lawn instead of the usual constant activity.

Ode to Life!

Everyone in Orange County had been told to stay in their house, away from their family and friends and to wear masks when they went outside. Some stood in line for food and other necessities. All businesses were closed except those deemed *essential*. "These measures are," everyone around the world was told, "*for your own good.*"

The interviews for the book were conducted outdoors, all wearing masks and sitting six feet or more apart...Until Gordon had to attend his brother's wedding in Nevada (he was the best man) and no one wore a mask! Before this book could be completed, Gordon had to be tested for Covid-19 twice, and wait the mandatory 14 days in self-quarantine each time. The second time it was because Gordon's wife, Barbara (83 years old at the time) had come down with the disease and was in ICU in a nearby hospital.

The interviews and book were completed virtually to protect the health of the Hoffmans, since Gordon eventually was diagnosed with Covid as well.

***

Something seemed too familiar to Eveline. She could not shake the feeling of being very scared and anxious. She took solace in the fact that she was at home with the first and only love of her life. Both she and her husband had been through much worse. They had beaten death, among other obstacles. They had stood in lines to get gas in the 1970s. They had kept their children inside on school days because of poison air around Los Angeles. They took extra precautions during pandemics and gladly were inoculated for polio or other diseases when vaccines became available.

Like every Jewish person they had celebrated Passover with their family, and knew the symbolic significance of having to stay indoors for a period of time, allowing the Angel of Death to pass by and fulfill the covenant that Jews had made with Yahweh (the nickname given to the Creator because Jews were not allowed to speak, let alone write the Creator's name).

Both Eveline and her husband Eddy had seen, done and been asked to do much worse to stay alive than merely wearing face-masks and regularly washing hands for protection from an unseen danger.

***

Without going into too much detail, Germany agreed to pay reparations to all those who had suffered at their hands in the Holocaust. Ed is still receiving quarterly payments from Germany and a stipend in his military pension for having been a Holocaust victim who enlisted after liberation. Eveline also received one payment from France for her treatment at the beginning of WWII. Her sister Jacqueline had gone after the money owed on behalf of herself and her two sisters.

No amount of money could ever make up for what either of them experienced.

Reparations for both African Slaves and the Indigenous Americans who had been displaced by U.S. empire building was still a hot topic of conversations in the United

States at the time of the quarantine. The topic of systemic racism, discrimination, and abuse as well as what to do about it in American Society continues to be hotly debated.

***

Eddy missed not being able to go to the Jewelry Shop, and Eveline was unable to work with her theater groups.

However, the two them were able to manage and deal with the daily challenges of staying Covid free. Eveline had a small anxiety attack with people handling food at Trader Joe's without gloves, but not to the extent she had felt when she realized she was a Holocaust survivor.

Eveline took special precautions with Eddy and wouldn't let him leave the car IF she allowed him to ride along on a short trip. The phone became a lifeline to friends and family. Discussions with others and each other became even more interesting and detailed with one caveat: When it comes to anyone other than Eddy and Eveline, there was NO discussion of politics! Eveline had found that people had become more and more staunch in their views. People, she felt, were talking at and to one another sometimes in heated arguments, not willing to hear what the other person was saying.

When the first full lockdown officially began in California, it was March 1st, 2020. Eveline was 83 years old.

It was her birthday.

as told to Gordon Richiusa

Afterword

A Final Statement by Eveline and Eddy Hoffman

We're not writers, but we have been asked to say a few words about what we wanted this book to accomplish.

Primarily this book is dedicated to our family. We want our children and grandchildren to know where they came from, to understand what has contributed to making them who they are or are *not*.

We also want our children to know what we've gone through, and why *we* are the way we are, why we've acted the way we have toward them, and how we've come to see life the way that we do. In addition to this dedication to our family, we want to add that we are both 100% American, because we are American by choice. It's different if you were born here. You had no choice, you got lucky.

We both really appreciate the freedom in this country that helped us to establish ourselves. We have made a good living and had a good life.

We think of ourselves as free, because we don't have anyone interfering with the choices that we make. Here in the states we've never had to be afraid of those choices. We didn't have to look over our shoulders. This is the kind of freedoms we're talking about that we didn't have until we came to this country. In most other countries you don't get that type of freedom.

Also, we both lived under more than one form of government including communism, fascism, a monarchy, a dictatorship, and we both wish people in this country would learn what can happen under a dictatorship to take away simple freedoms.

It's too bad that in public schools it's not compulsory for every student to learn about the history of our government and other countries' governments. It should also be compulsory to learn about the Holocaust, and that it wasn't just the Jews who were put into concentration camps. There were even Germans, both criminals and political dissidents.

It seems like some people don't understand what it all means. You cannot necessarily read a few paragraphs from history books to really make the connection between what happened before and what is going on in the world today.

Perhaps there is too much of a me-me-me in today's society. Our hope is that this book may help to enlighten people a little bit, teach people to want to expand their horizons and look not only at what is happening right in front of them, but how things come about.

Human beings probably learn best by just listening to stories and by taking advantage of the experiences of others. In this book we're able to tell our stories, as we've done for a while. Someone else is putting the words together for us. We hope everyone appreciates the effort.

When we speak at schools people of all ages come up to us and say, "Oh my God! It's real!" That sends a chill up our spines! When you read about something it's just a story, but when you meet the people who are telling you their own story and what they've actually gone through, and they share it in a natural and not a rehearsed way, it brings the story to life. In this case we want to bring the story of the Holocaust to life, but also the wide-ranging effects that these inhumane atrocities have had.

We don't have a script. We just talk and let others talk. When they talk, we listen. That's what people relate to. The kids just flock around us, and they want to ask questions when it's all over. *Can I take a picture with you? How did you really feel?* All of a sudden they're asking questions, showing that the stories have sparked the desire to learn. Sometimes they just want to shake our hands. They have stood in long lines just to shake our hands.

Others have more to ask. The question we are most often asked, in person or in the hundreds of letters that we have received, is, *"Do you hate the Germans?"*

The answer we give is this, *"No, we don't hate the Germans."* We probably will never be able to totally forgive those who mistreated us and other Jews, those Germans for what they did, and we'll never be able to say that we are not still feeling the affects, but those feelings hurt us more than anyone.

There's a saying: *"Hatred corrodes the container it's held in."* If you keep hate in you, it eats you up. Telling our story has been eye opening for all of us.

Some people are always complaining. We don't understand that. When Eddy was drafted he couldn't believe the amount of complaining that soldiers did. They got good wages by his standards and had no expenses. He was happy in the military, because he had seen a lot worse than just taking a few orders and felt he owed allegiance to the country that freed him.

Whatever we've had to do, we did it with pleasure or at least we did our best. We stuck to what was needed to be accomplished. We've done so many things in our lives, changed so many trades, lived full lives together and have learned that the most valuable trait one can have is adaptability.

We adjusted to all the changes and circumstances in our lives. It was never, "Oh poor me, now I have to do this or that." We faced every challenge without self-pity.

You know, we humans can do anything when we put our minds to it. Trouble is we usually have to get to be middle-aged or past to learn this lesson. On the other hand, some things seem obvious throughout. We've always felt that wars are bad and that we need to stop having them. We know we have to protect ourselves from outside enemies, but we also have to protect ourselves from enemies within.

We believe that humans are evolving. The average person is good, but there are always some bad ones who seem to ruin it for the rest of us. Even the cavemen, we're sure there were some nice ones and some nasty ones. That's the way humans are.

Another lesson we've learned is how humans react to trauma. When a person experiences trauma of any sort, that's when your survival instincts kick in. You really don't know how you're going to react to trauma until it happens to you. You might believe that you'll react a certain way, *"Oh, I'll do this or I would have done that,"* but maybe you won't do any of the things you thought or maybe you'll just freeze.

Other people experience an obstacle and BOOM, they go over it, but you truly don't know. Maybe the kinder the person you are, the more you've learned about yourself, the more you've experienced the goodness of others, then these things will help you in those moments of trauma. Those are the moments when you just have to react to survive.

Today, we both volunteer doing what we can to help others, especially those who are struggling. We have to help each other. We are not alone. We know we are always dependent on everybody else.

When you are retired and live in a community like we're in, you have less stress generally than you had when you were younger. You don't have to worry about putting kids through school or taking care of a household. Everything that we used to worry about is done. Now we can just be. It's just wonderful.

Ode to Life!

Now we can look at people in a different way. We don't have to worry about whether we suspect or fear them. We can enjoy people and each other without suspicion, without worrying about what the other person wants to get from us. We don't have to worry about the boss, the bills, whatever. Now we're a lot older and we look at our lives and think, *"We wish life could be much longer,"* but since it can't be, we enjoy every single day.

One of our neighbors is 111 years old. He's the oldest male in the United States. Eddy takes him bread every week. The man doesn't need it; he's very well to do, but that's not the point. The point is love. He's gotten to that age, an age when you really desire and need human contact, but people don't visit him anymore. They don't bother with him. He tells Eddy, "The only person coming to see me is YOU."

This innate quality of wanting to do something for others is not what helped either one of us survive or has drawn us to one another. We both like ourselves and each other, because we are true to ourselves and know that the other person has those qualities we respect. Each of us feels lucky and satisfied to have found the other.

Before we met neither wanted to get married. We both thought marriage would interfere with life plans. What we found was that it's possible to find someone who makes an individual life plan easier to accomplish because the other individual believes the same things.

Finally, we both believe that each person must be their own best example. We have tried to teach our children to be honest with themselves and to like themselves.

Whatever you do in anything including business, be honest and straight-forward. Don't ever underestimate any other person, ever. We're not saying live only for today. We have to look at tomorrow, but when the opportunity arises to just enjoy, don't negate it.

If a trip comes up and you can possibly do it then drop everything and go. Later on in life you may want to do that same thing and you won't be able to, prevented by sickness or something else. There are things we don't experience and when we're older we regret it. Chances don't always come up again. Don't pass up any opportunity to enjoy life. Take advantage of what life has to offer.

People seem to be drawn to our optimism, just as much as this quality has drawn us together. This is what makes us compatible. We allow the other person to be their own person, without us always having to agree.

Ode to Life!

as told to Gordon Richiusa

Timeline Explanation

Eddy and Eveline's story, as with the many memoirs and recollections of Holocaust survivors is not only true but has taken place in some of the most significant moments of human history. A full Human Discrimination Timeline is presented here with significant dates displayed.

The main characters in this book, Eddy and Eveline Hoffman are a married couple for over sixty three years. Both are Jewish Holocaust survivors, alive and well at the time of this writing (2020).

Eddy Hoffman was fourteen years old when he was taken into the German Killing Camp known as Auschwitz, for no other reason but his family was Jewish. His thirty-six year old mother, his grandfather and his youngest brother Tibor were all killed immediately upon arrival. He lost all of his immediate family there.

Eveline was only five years old at the same time as Eddy's abduction and slavery. She was one of three sisters, abandoned by their parents as they were also threatened with death for being Jewish. Though the girls were in hiding in the south of France, then in Barcelona, Spain, the three children made a harrowing escape to the United States, where all Eveline's immediate family survived their ordeal and were later reunited. Sister Paulette died of a rare and aggressive form of colon cancer in August of 2013. She is missed everyday.

Human Discrimination Development Timeline

--40,000 BC evidence of humans in Europe

--*23,000 BC* humans inhabit North America

--*4000-6000* BC Humans inhabit Asian Continent

—2000 BC According to Torah Abraham founded Judaism

--*985 A.D* Norse settlement founded on Greenland (part of North America)

--*400 A.D.* Hawaiian Islands inhabited

--*1758* August 29, colonists established the first Indian reservation

--*1830* May 28, the Indian Removal Act was signed by President Jackson

--1861 U.S. Civil War began

--1865 Lincoln assassinated April 15

--1865 *December 6*, the 13th amendment abolished slavery in the United States

--1866 The Civil Rights Act made blacks full U.S. citizens (and this repealed the Dred Scott
   decision).

--1868 The 14th Amendment granted full U.S. citizenship to African-Americans.

--1870 The 15th amendment, ratified in , extended the right to vote to black males.

--1889 Adolf Hitler born in Austria, April 20

--1893 On Jan. 17, Hawaii's monarchy was overthrown when a group of businessmen and sugar planters forced Queen Liliuokalani to abdicate

--1901 Eddy's father was born.

--1907 Eddy's mother was born. Maiden name Frid.

--1914 Austrian Archduke Franz and wife Sophie were assassinated 28 June in Bosnia, by a 19-year-old Bosnian Serb, Gavrilo Princip.

--1919 Salvatore Richiusa born (December 11)

--1920 Women get the right to vote (August 18)

--1920 Nazi party founded in Germany (February 24th, in Munich)

--1921 Flora Mae Villani born: Oct. 7

--1923 Hitler attempted to seize power in a failed coup in Munich

--1924 Native people won citizenship in the U.S.

--1925 Volume 1 of Mein Kampf was published

--1929-Adolf (Eddy) Hoffman is Born-- February 21

--1933 President Paul von Hindenburg appoints Adolf Hitler as Chancellor on 30 January

--1937 Eddy Hoffman Had a Dream

--1937 Eveline is born (March 1st)

--1937 Volkswagon founded as Gesellschaft zur Vorbereitung des Deutschen Volkswagens mbH

--1938 'Volkswagenwerk GmbH' initial logo comprised of the 'Nazi' flag designed in the shape of a swastika symbol.

--1939 The Hungarian army, allied with Germany's Third Reich, marched into Eddy's town. (March 15, 1939)

--1939 Britain and France declare war on Germany 03 September

Ode to Life!

--1940 Nazis invade France.

--1941 U.S. Military is attacked at Pearl Harbor Japanese Imperial Navy (Dec. 7)

--1942 Eddy and Isadore sold stamped postcards to military. Paid in money or BREAD...Eddy gave it to his family

--1942 February 19, Roosevelt signed Executive Order 9006, which led to Japanese Americans being interred in prison camps. (Canada soon followed suit, relocating 21,000 of its Japanese residents from its west coast. Mexico enacted its own version, and eventually 2,264 more people of Japanese descent were removed from Peru, Brazil, Chile and Argentina to the United States)

--1942, Christmas Eve a five year old Eveline and her two sisters are smuggled out of France by the *patois* (mountain people), over the Pyrenees to Spain.

--1943 Jews forced to wear Star of David and forced into Ghettos

--1943 Jacqueline, Eveline, Paulette smuggled out of Europe on Sera Pinta from Portugal along with 60 other children of the Holocaust

--1945 April US forces liberate the Buchenwald concentration camp near Weimar

--1945 May 6, Eddy Hoffman was liberated with the help of Patton's 3rd Division.

--1945 May 23 Third Reich officially ceased to exist.

—1945 August 6 first atomic bomb ever used in war was dropped on Hiroshima, Japan/ August 9 second atomic bomb (and last ever used in war) was dropped on Nagasaki, Japan by the U.S

--1945 Sept. 2 WWII Ended Officially

--1945 October 24, The United Nations Officially came into existence

--1945 Eddy's Aunt RE-married and moved to Hoffman Falau area, village, with new husband.

—1947 Eddy decides to move from Glasgow to London

--1948 January 30, Mahatma Gandhi assassinated

--1948 May, Israel becomes a country

--1949 During a period of rationing in London, Eddy takes out a bakery license.

--1950-51 Eddy had own business in London

--1951 Eveline returned to U.S. from Paris, France.

--1952 Eddy came to the United States and was drafted into 101st Airborne Division.

--1953 Sent to S. Carolina, Third Army

--1953 Eddy in Fort Bragg N. Carolina, asked Captain to send him overseas. He didn't want to teach baking.

--1954 Eddy in Hokkaido, Japan

--1954 Eddy went back to baking; A worker there was the sister of the blacksmith in Eddy's hometown. "So you're Mrs. Pops' sister?"

--1954 Eddy discharged

--1955 Eveline graduated high school, Eveline met Eddy.

--1957 Hoffmans married June 30 in a double wedding with sister Paulette and brother in law Eddie Schlechter

--1958 Hoffmans had a bakery (less than a year).

--1958-59 Eveline wanted to help father, in Philadelphia

--1959-60 Eddy becomes a furrier, Eveline worked for Indussa, lived in Queens near Van Wyck Expressway.

--1959 August 21, Hawaii becomes the 50th U.S. State

Ode to Life!

--1961 Hoffmans moved to San Francisco, March.
—1961 April 9 Joseph Gregory Hoffman was born
--1961 August 4 Barack Obama born in Honolulu, Hawaii
—1961 August 13 Construction of the Berlin Wall began
--1962 Native Americans were finally guaranteed the right to vote in every state
—1962 December 14. Suzanne born
--1964 Eddy invited to Reservation by a Native American Friend for Thanksgiving Dinner
—1965 August 10 Carla Jeanne born
--1965 August 11 Watts Riots began--In the *DogHouse*
—1966 Eddy and Eveline opened up *Chez Edouard*
--1968 April Martin Luther King Jr. Assassinated
--1968 John Robert Kennedy Assassinated
—1969 David Leonard born September 18
—1972 Closed down *Chez Eduard*
—1973 Eddy took over Redwood House
—1973 Hoffmans went to Israel
—1974 Eddy took over *Proto Tools*
—1975 Tour of Greece, Rome, Switzerland, England
—1976 Eddy asked to take over the Original *PANTRY*/ bought *Tridair* which Eveline ran.
---1977,8,9. Sold Proto Tool and ran Tridair cafeteria with Eveline.
—1980 Moved to Palos Verdes Eveline started going to Jenny Craig
--1980 John Lennon assassinated (Dec. 8)
—1981-83 Eveline asked to work for Jenny Craig (San Pedro)

--1984 Indira Gandhi assassinated (Oct. 31)

—1987-88 Eveline diagnosed with breast cancer, had mastectomy (reconstructive surgery)

—1989 November 1 Berlin Wall falls. In Palos Verdes at the time...Had strong emotional reaction... "They have no idea what that means." Eddy said. Eveline took out small Statue of Liberty and was crying.

—1991 Eddy's Aunt killed by SCUD missiles in Tel Aviv

—1992 Eveline started working for Jenny Craig full time.

—1992 Ed retired from Business. Took job with Honey Baked Ham, as production manager.

--*1993 **The Apology Resolution*** passed by the United States Congress is acknowledged that the overthrow of the Kingdom of Hawaii in 1893 was an illegal act

—2001 TWIN TOWERS ATTACKED (September 11)

*Hoffmans babysitting in San Diego, Colin (grandson Carla's first born). As Colin grew he had always shown a special interest in his grandparents' past and would ask non-stop questions of every detail.

--2002 Eddy started taking Jewelry classes at El Camino College

—2004 Hoffmans move to Laguna Woods Village Sept. 19th

—2007, 8,9 stopped working for Jenny Craig joined theater group.

--2009 January 20, President Obama Inaugurated for the 1st time. Both Hoffmans voted for him.

Ode to Life!

—2010 Eveline diagnosed with multiple myeloma (February) and had bone marrow transplant 10 months later.

—2010 October pre-bone marrow transplant/treatment party

--2011 May 2 Osama bin Laden killed

—2013 January 20 President Obama Inaugurated for the second time in a private official ceremony taking place the next day (21st).

--2012,13,14,15,16 White suprematist activity and antisemitic hate crimes on the rise worldwide.

--2016 December 7, Michelle Manu is first woman inducted into King Kamehameha's Royal order on Oahu, after having danced hula on the beach at Hickam Field wearing original Two-Hearts-As-One bracelet on one arm and Eddy Hoffman's copper version on the other.

—2017 January 20, President Trump was inaugurated . Both Hoffmans voted for him.

--2018 December 29, Ed donates the copper version of Two Hearts As One Bracelet once worn by Michelle Manu to Museum of Tolerance (Rabbi Cooper).

--2020 February, Coronavirus pandemic causes worldwide sequestering and growing calls for self-sequestering, locked borders, and Asian discrimination become commonplace while Anti-semitism is once again on the rise.

—2020 March-June Sequestering rules are relaxed slightly. Rioting takes place around country when a white police officer in Minnesota kills a black man George Floyd by kneeing on his neck. The officer and four others who watched were fired and are being prosecuted.

--2020 September 18 Supreme Court Justice Ruth Bader-Ginsburg Dies at age 87 of pancreatic cancer.

Ode to Life!

as told to Gordon Richiusa

PHOTO GALLERY

From Left to Right: Anna, Paulette, Jacqueline, Eveline, and Simon Grossman

From Left to Right: Carl, Szeren, Tibby (Bottom) Adolph/Eddy (Top Middle), and Josef Hoffman

Ode to Life!

Child Holocaust survivors Eddy Hoffman (top row right) handwritten notations across photo margin

Military Intelligence, 1953. Eddy Hoffman top row, second from right end

as told to Gordon Richiusa

Michelle Manu, at 75th Anniversary of Pearl Harbor attack (photo taken at Hickam Field beach, Oahu) wears and dances hula with Eddy's original Hoffman Copper bracelet and the original Two-Hearts-Beating-As-One (Heroes' Hearts) bracelet made by Salvatore Richiusa from a downed Japanese plane from the Pearl Harbor battle.

Ode to Life!

At Eddy Hoffman's 90th birthday party, from Left to Right: Grandson Canyon, Daughter Carla, Grandson Colin, Son Joe, Eveline, Daughter Suzanne, Eddy, Son David

as told to Gordon Richiusa

Eveline Hoffman holding the handmade star her mother gave her

At his beloved Jewelry shop Eddy Hoffman (L) receives Aloha Award from Heroes' Hearts Director Gordon Richiusa (R)

Ode to Life!

Eddy Hoffman (L) gives a copper "Heroes' Hearts" to Rabbi Abraham Cooper at Museum of Tolerance office

Eddy and Eveline Hoffman on their wedding day.

as told to Gordon Richiusa

www.ingramcontent.com/pod-product-compliance
Lightning Source LLC
Chambersburg PA
CBHW032302300426
44110CB00033B/274